A Good Horse
Is Never a Bad Color

A Good Horse
Is Never a Bad Color

Mark Rashid

Illustrations by Herb Mignery

Johnson Books
Boulder

Spring Creek Press
Estes Park

In memory of Robert J. "Wrangler Rob" Kralovec, my friend.
March 5, 1959–February 11, 1995

Published in the United States by Johnson Books, a Division of Johnson Publishing Company, 1880 South 57th Court, Boulder, Colorado 80301.

9 8 7

Illustrations by Herb Mignery

Horse training, clinics, equine rehabilitation,
and other services provided by Mark Rashid
can be arranged by writing Mark at
P.O. Box 3241, Estes Park, CO 80517.
Comments about this book are also welcome.

Library of Congress Cataloging-in-Publication Data
Rashid, Mark
  A good horse is never a bad color / Mark Rashid ; illustrations by Herb Mignery.
    p.   cm.
  Includes bibliographical references and index.
  ISBN 1-55566-142-4 (alk. paper)
  1. Horses—Training.   2. Horses—Behavior.   3. Horses—Psychology.
4. Horses—United States —Anecdotes.   I. Title.
SF287.R265   1996
636.1—dc20   95-51232
                                                                  CIP

Printed in the United States by
Johnson Printing
1880 South 57th Court
Boulder, Colorado 80301

 Printed on recycled paper with soy ink

Contents

Foreword

ONE OF THE truly great things about working for a horse publication is being able to work with, and absorb, the ideas and philosophies of some of the most gifted trainers in the country. In editing their articles for publication, I get to climb into their brains for a while and "hang out"—always directly applying some aspect of their teaching to something I'm currently going through, or have experienced in the past, with one of my own horses.

Somewhere in my filing cabinet is a picture of Mark Rashid, walking toward the camera, shoulder to shoulder with an unrestrained horse. The overall impression this snapshot gives is one of equal partners who have just finished working for the day and are headed home for "a beer and a bite to eat." Such is a relationship that is based on mutual respect and trust. It focuses not as much on performance as on a horse's understanding of what is being asked of him and his willingness to accept that request.

For the most part, in this book as well as in his first one, Mark's equine clientele are not the coddled, push-button, want-for-nothing-in-their-lives, pedigreed show stock that most trainers focus on. Rather, through his work with the Colorado Horse Rescue and similar facilities, Mark seems to draw in more than his share of damaged and wary equine goods. These are horses that, as he states in the book, are not so much physically abused as they are mentally "spoiled." (Funny, we seem to use that word only when we mean over-indulged.) In fact, if these horses were humans, Mark would be more of a social worker/psychologist than a teacher, running a halfway house for the criminally mistrained and misunderstood.

Take the title chapter of "A Good Horse Is Never a Bad Color," for example. In it, Mark tells of his work with horses of the Arabian, paint, and appaloosa persuasions. While their training problems were considerable and quite genuine, each also suffered, to some degree, from prejudiced and stereotypical thinking regarding their breed in general.Who among us, who has owned a horse of one of these breeds, has not had to endure censure and I-told-you-so's across the back fence from self-righteous, opinionated, horse snobs?

It is Mark's contention that, in most cases of bad equine behavior, it is the human's poor understanding of a particular breed or horse that has caused the problem to develop.

Quite a while back, I saw something listed in the local want-ads that I felt warranted checking out. It read: "Six-year-old Hanoverian gelding for sale. Athletic and hauls well. $1800." Although I wasn't in the market for another horse, my sister was. Being a three-day-eventer, she is particularly partial to the German warmblood breed known as the Hanoverian. These animals are in great demand as dressage and jumping prospects, due to their large but athletic frame and pleasant disposition. What, I idly wondered, was a member of such an exotic breed doing way out here in cowboy country?

The gelding was saddled and waiting for me when I arrived. A gorgeous but sweating dapple-gray, standing just shy of sixteen hands, he was smaller and somewhat more refined than the Hanoverians I was used to seeing, but beautifully conformed and in good flesh. I was informed that he had been bred and trained at a local thoroughbred farm, then sold when he failed to grow to Olympic proportions. The current owner had bought him as a weekend roping horse, but said that he couldn't give the gelding the exercise he seemed to require. I tried to imagine this powerhouse before me standing idly at one end of the roping arena, waiting perhaps all day for his one or two chances to move out.

I moved to the horse, speaking to him as I stroked him, in preparation for taking a "test" ride. The horse gave no indication that he heard or felt me. He stood stoically still, his eyes focused on a distant mountain. The owner said he had warmed him up by lunging him a while. Normally, I ask to see an owner ride a horse first, so I can watch how the animal behaves under saddle. However, I happened to notice the cast on the owner's arm and sensed a bit of reluctance on his part to mount the animal. So, without further ado, I set a foot in the stirrup and prepared to swing my leg over.

No sooner had my weight come to rest in the saddle than several things happened in quick succession. First, I felt every muscle in the gelding's back contract into what felt like a huge fist with a saddle strapped to it. At the same time, I was aware of a staccato, dancing action from all four of his feet. Third, I got a good look at the heavy steel railing of the round pen we were in. What had seemed to be an adequately-sized space for riding was now rapidly closing in, until it appeared to be only about ten feet in diameter. Various bells, whistles, and alarms, as well as flashing red railroad lights, were going off inside my head. I swung back down to stand firmly before the owner and said, "Now, maybe you should tell me something about this horse."

The owner proceeded to tell me how the horse had "just up and soured all of a sudden." After the particularly violent episode that broke his arm, he had started actively campaigning for a new owner. "I just want my money back out of him, that's all," he assured me.

Needless to say, I passed on the horse. At the time, I racked my brain for someone to send that poor animal to for retraining (or at least a better attitude). It was quite obvious that his problems stemmed from human error. Had I known about Mark Rashid back then, I would have bought the gelding and hauled him up to Colorado myself.

I happened to run into the owner of the Hanoverian many months later, and learned what became of him. A bunch of local cowhands hauled the horse out into the desert and took turns trying to "buck him out," which they couldn't seem to accomplish. Then one of the hands took him down to Phoenix and tried to sell him to a rodeo livestock dealer, as a potential bucking horse. Word had it that, when he couldn't get enough money for him at the rodeo, the kid just decided to "chow" him at a local auction.

Sad stories such as this one point out the fact that we still have a lot to learn about the magnificent animal we call the horse. All of us need to give thanks for trainers, like Mark Rashid, who have devoted their lives to helping us gain that knowledge and understanding. The sooner we all get educated, the better the horses of this world will fare.

Indeed, a good horse is never a bad color (except maybe after a hard rain and a good roll in the paddock). And you can bet that, hidden inside every supposed "problem" horse, there is a good one just waiting to come out.

Bonnie Ebsen-Jackson, Editor
The Western Horse magazine
Prescott, Arizona

Preface

THIS BOOK WAS started back in the late 1800s by someone other than me.

Oh, I suppose an argument can be made that I am the one who wrote it simply because I'm the one who put the pencil to paper, as it were. But I don't really see it that way.

I met the fellow who I consider to be the author in the mid-1960s. I wasn't much more than a sprout at the time. He was a kind old man in his seventies who ran a little horse operation not far from where I grew up. He offered me a non-paying job one day after he caught me sneaking around one of his pastures. The job was little more than mucking out corrals and stalls, but I felt it was a better choice than being arrested for trespassing. Little did I know that the kind old man would turn out to be one of the finest horsemen I would ever have the honor to meet.

Now, there are horsemen and there are *horsemen*. He was the latter. He had the uncanny ability to get a horse, any horse, to do whatever it was he wanted, whether that was catching one that didn't want to be caught, riding one that couldn't be ridden, or shoeing one that didn't want to be shod. He could always find a way to get the job done. The thing that was so unusual about him, though, was that I never once saw him raise his hand to a horse nor did I ever hear him raise his voice. He simply had a way with horses, some people might even say—a gift.

I guess it would have been easy for him to go about his business without giving me a second thought. But that wasn't his way. As time went on, he found ways to teach me about horses and his method of working with them. He taught me that before we can expect a horse to work well for us, it must first trust in us. If we can find a way to gain its trust, respect is sure to follow.

He had a theory—that all horses are born good, no matter what breed, size, or color they happen to be. It's only what we do with them after they're born that determines whether they'll remain good or not. I think he made it his goal in life to make sure that any horse he came in contact with remained a good horse. It was a goal that he passed along to me.

He was a man of few words, but the few words he did speak often contained volumes. There is one particular example that I recall. It was at the end of a very long, frustrating afternoon when I'd been trying to teach a young horse I was riding how to go from a trot to a lope. Nothing that I'd done worked. In fact, it had gotten to the point where the more that I insisted he perform, the harder he fought me.

The old man approached me after I finally quit for the day and asked rather nonchalantly if I'd be interested in learning the secret to being a good horse trainer. The instant I said I would, he clenched his fist and held it in front of my face.

"Get me to open my fist," he said bluntly.

With that, I pinched, pulled, and pried with all my might trying to get him to open his gnarled hand. Nothing worked. Unable to get his fist open after several minutes, I finally gave up. He slowly lowered his arm and said simply, "Maybe you should have asked."

No, I don't see myself as the author of this book. It was written for me. I was simply the one who got to put it to paper.

I hope you enjoy it as much as I have.

PART ONE

The Idea

1

The Horseman from Wyoming

IT WAS ONLY 10:30 in the morning, but it felt like I'd already put in a full day. It had all started about two hours earlier as I rode my bike up the gravel road to the little horse ranch where I worked. I may have only been twelve years old at the time but as I neared the ranch gate, I could see right off that I was in trouble.

I'd been the last one through the gate the night before, and while I was sure I had closed it, I knew as I approached that I hadn't latched it. I was sure of this because the eighteen horses that were normally in the front pasture of the ranch were no longer there. Instead, they were strung out for about a mile and a half along the ditch at the side of the road, happily munching the lush green grass that grew there.

Parked in front of the wide-open gate was my boss's 1949 Ford pickup truck. And there, sitting on the passenger-side running board, was my boss, Walter Pruit. A filterless Camel cigarette hung precariously from his lips, and he was just finishing it as I approached.

I skidded my bike to a stop near the back of the old, beat-up pickup, terrified of what the old man might do or say to me because of my unforgivable mistake. At the very least, I figured my days of working for him were over. My biggest concern, however, was not so much that he was going to fire me (after all, I wasn't getting paid anyway), but how he was going to do it. Would he just flat out fire me and send me packing, or would I be chastised and flogged first?

From his seat on the running board, the old man slowly glanced up at me, took the last drag from his cigarette and dropped it on the ground. He mashed the smoldering butt with the toe of his boot. It was quite obvious, by the number of already mashed cigarette butts at his feet, that he had been sitting there for quite a while. After stomping out the cigarette, he slowly rose to his feet and faced me, shaking his head. He took one step toward me, then reached inside the box of the pickup.

Here it comes, I thought to myself. He's probably got a baseball bat in there that he'll whack me in the head with. Proper punishment for such a heinous crime, I guessed.

I prepared for the worst as he pulled his hand out of the pickup box. Much to my surprise, all he had was a halter and lead rope that he brought over and handed to me. He went back to the pickup and pulled out a pile of seventeen more, which he brought over and dropped at my feet. Then, without saying a word, he walked over and climbed into the cab of the pickup. He sat for a few seconds while he lit up another cigarette before trying to start the old truck.

After several unsuccessful attempts, the old Ford finally wheezed and coughed to life. He began to ease the truck down the quarter-mile long driveway that led to the barn, the truck sounding all the way like a cross between a steam-powered thrashing machine and a bulldozer with a bad muffler.

He had no sooner pulled away than a light rain began to fall. Not wanting to spend all day in the rain catching horses, I quickly leaned my bicycle up against the fence and got down to the business at hand. Luckily, the horse nearest to me was an old gelding named Mac who had little or no ambition to do anything but stand still and eat. As a result, he allowed me to walk right up and catch him. I slid the halter on and began to walk him back to the gate, followed closely by Mac's best buddy, another old gelding named Blaze.

Just like that I had two horses caught and returned to the pasture.

Great, I thought. This is going to be easy. Only sixteen more to go. The horses, however, had other ideas. As I began to make my way toward the next horse, a young mare named Lucky, she suddenly raised her head, snorted, and ran across the road into a large hay field. One by one each of the other horses followed until all sixteen were running back and forth, kicking and playing, tails and heads high, through the field.

For the next hour, as the rain fell harder, I followed the herd while they ran first one way, then the other. Luckily, the field was fenced on three sides so at least they were in somewhat of an enclosure and were content to stay there. Otherwise, I'd probably still be trying to catch them. I had to admit, as I sloshed through puddles in the freshly cut hayfield, that I wished I had a bucket full of grain to assist me. Surely, they'd all come to the sound of grain shaking in a bucket. Unfortunately, that was simply not an option. The old man wouldn't allow any of his horses to be coerced into being caught with such a cheap and unimaginative trick.

"You shouldn't own horses," I had heard him say a hundred times, "if you can't catch 'em."

It took a while, but finally some of the more out-of-shape horses began to play out and allow me to approach and halter them. Fifteen minutes later, the rest of them also settled down and allowed themselves to be caught and returned to the pasture. Finally, after over an hour-and-a-half's worth of catching horses, I was able to start my morning chores. My chores consisted mainly of feeding, watering, and cleaning up after the twenty or so horses that stayed in the corrals and paddocks up near the barn. I was also in charge of tending to horses that happened to be in any of the six box stalls inside the barn, all of which were empty at that time. This was great luck, seeing's how I was terribly late getting started in the first place. With everything I had to tend to outside, I probably wouldn't have gotten to anything inside for another hour.

Like a man possessed, I flew around the place feeding, watering, and cleaning, all the while getting drenched by what now seemed like nothing short of a monsoon. Because of my blistering pace, I was able to finish my chores in what felt like record time. After finishing up at the last corral, I burst into the tack room to announce to the old man that my chores were finally finished, only to find him not there.

The tack room was a sixteen-by-sixteen-foot room that had been added to the main barn, it seemed, as an afterthought. In it were several saddle stands with saddles and blankets, a small work bench, a potbellied wood stove, and the old man's favorite chair. Bridles, cinches, halters, and the like hung in various places on the wall and were in no particular order. The room had three doors—the one that I'd just come through, leading to the outside, one on the left, which led to the main barn, and one on the right, which opened into a large box stall the old man used as a foaling stall. The room had a very distinctive odor to it, an interesting mixture of leather, horse sweat, and cigarette smoke.

As I stood in the tack room door, I heard what sounded like running water—not running water from a spigot or water faucet, but from something much bigger, like a river or waterfall. This sound wouldn't have bothered me if I were in the woods or near a large body of running water. Unfortunately, I was near neither. In fact, the sound wasn't even coming from outside. It was coming from inside the main barn.

I walked over to the door and looked into the barn only to see the entire floor covered with about three inches of water. The only place that was relatively dry was a high spot in the middle of the barn where the old man was standing, hat tipped back, scratching his head.

He was staring up at a large hole in the roof where water from the storm outside was spilling through in truckloads. He stood there a few seconds longer, then turned and trudged through the water and past me into the tack room.

"I should'a had them boys fix that before they left," he said quietly.

The boys he was referring to were a couple of fellows in their late teens who had been working for him since before I'd started working at the place two years earlier. As near as I could tell, he even paid them. One's name was Mike, the other's name was Spitter.

Now, while I was fairly certain that "Spitter" was not the name his mother gave him when he was born, for the life of me, I couldn't figure out why everybody called him that. I hadn't ever seen him spit, not anymore than normal, that is, and he didn't drool or slobber much. I guess it was just one of those nicknames that someone had adorned him with at some point in time, and for some unfortunate reason, it stuck.

Spitter and Mike did all the really hard work on the place—all the work that the old man had trouble doing because he was too old and I had trouble doing because I was too young. They did most of the riding of the young colts, under the watchful eye of the old man. They also did all major fence work, kept the well working properly, did tack repair, ran the tractor and manure spreader, and did all the maintenance on the barn and other buildings on the place. This included repairing the barn roof when it sprung one of its periodic leaks, which were more common than not. In fact, they had just finished repairing one such leak when one of them stepped on another soft spot, causing the roof to give way and creating the hole through which Mother Nature was now filling the barn with barrel after barrel of water. Unfortunately, before they could get around to fixing the hole, Mike got drafted into the Army. Spitter, being his best friend and not wanting him to go into the Army alone, signed up and went with him. That had been almost two months earlier. We never did see either one of them again.

The old man walked over and sat down in his chair. As he began to pry one of his rubber boots (the kind with the buckles down the front) off his foot with the toe of the other, I meekly told him how sorry I was for forgetting to latch the gate.

"I'll tell you something," he said with a slight grin. "You're not the first person that ever left a gate open." The boot popped off his foot and landed on the floor in front of him. "And you sure won't be the last."

He sat back in his chair and looked straight at me. "The important thing is that we didn't lose any stock. What happened to you," he continued, as he leaned forward and began prying the other rubber boot off, "wasn't that big of a deal. Heck, I remember one time when I was your age, maybe a little younger, I forgot to latch the gate on a pen full of horses that my dad and his hired hand had just spent three days gathering." He shook his head as the other boot popped off. "I had horses scattered all over the damn prairie."

Then something very strange happened, something that had never happened before. The old man settled back in his chair. He got very quiet for a few seconds. Then out of the blue, he began talking about his past. He told me that he was born somewhere in Nebraska, in 1896 or '95, he wasn't sure, and that shortly afterwards his family moved west to Wyoming, where he lived until he was seventeen. He said that his dad originally tried to raise cattle after the move but found that the large cattle operations in the area had a monopoly on the business. For that reason, his dad switched over to horses. When he was five or six years old, an old Indian came looking for work and his dad hired him.

"We all called him Tom," the old man said, "but I don't guess that was his real name."

He said that he and Tom became very close and that it was Tom, not his father, who had taught him much of what he knew about horses. One of the very first things Tom had shown him was how a horse can use the length of his body to warm himself. He explained that right when the sun comes up, after a cool night, you will see horses standing with their entire sides toward the sun. By doing that, they can warm as much of their body as possible all at once. However, on hot days, horses usually stand with their backsides toward the sun, exposing the least amount of their body's surface to the sun and limiting the amount of heat their bodies take in.

He said that Tom showed him many of the little things about horses that no one else seemed to know. Tom even showed him how horses communicate with one another and how important it is for us to understand those things.

"Once you understand how a horse communicates," the old man said, as he lit another cigarette, "you can understand how he thinks. Once you understand how he thinks, you can understand what's important to him. And that's the key."

He nodded slowly while shaking the lit match until it was extinguished. The look on my face must have told him that his last statement went right over my head, so he went on to explain.

"Anybody can force a horse to do what they want," he continued. "But if you force him to do it, it won't be important to him to do it right. He'll do it almost right some of the time. He'll do just enough to get by. But if you show him what you want and then reward him when he does it just right, it will become important to him to do the thing right every time." He paused. "Understand?"

"I think so," I replied, after running the statement through my mind a few times.

He continued to talk for the better part of an hour, explaining how horses treat each other with respect and dignity that we, as humans, often don't even show to one another. The example he used was that most fights between horses stop before they start. Squealing and body language are usually enough of a deterrent that an argument never even comes to blows. In most cases, the less dominant horse will show respect by getting away from the more dominant one. The dominant horse leaves the other horse his dignity by allowing him to move away without further attack.

He then talked of the ways Tom showed him how to get more from a horse by using less.

"Why do people use spurs?" he asked abruptly.

"Um," I started, "to get their horses to go faster?"

"That's right," he said. "Let me ask you this. Did the Indians use spurs on their horses?"

I had to stop and think for a minute. I remembered looking at photographs and paintings of warriors on horseback and in none of the pictures did I recall any of them wearing spurs.

"No, they didn't."

"That's right," he said, shaking his head. "Some of the finest war horses in the world were ridden by the Plains Indians. They could run faster, turn quicker, stop shorter, and outdistance the U.S. Cavalry on just about any given day. The Cavalry boys had saddles, blankets, bridles with bits, and spurs on their boots. The Indians usually went bareback with nothing to stop and turn their horses with but a leather rope around the horse's neck or around his bottom jaw. They got more with less." He paused for a second, noticing that it had just stopped raining.

"You can't force a horse to be that way," he continued, rising from his chair and walking to the door. "They have to want to be that way. It had to be important for them to want to do those things, and the Indians knew how to do that."

He stuck his hand out the door, palm up, to double check whether raindrops were still falling. "While they were getting more with less," he said, bringing his arm back in and looking at the palm of his hand, "we were getting less with more and thought we were something special because of it."

He turned and looked me straight in the eye.

"Horses are good animals. They deserve better."

He turned and walked out the door with me hot on his heels. He made his way to the large sliding door in front of the barn and pushed it open.

The barn and the other buildings on the place were over sixty years old and were all relatively sound structurally except, of course, for the barn roof. At one time, the barn itself even had a hardwood floor. However, it had long since been removed, which left the dirt floor recessed by about four inches. That's why the floor flooded the way it did.

I went to the tool shed and brought back a couple of shovels. Then, while the old man and I began to dig some shallow trenches in order to drain the barn, he started once again to reminisce about his past.

He told me that he was riding horses almost before he could walk, as did most kids of that time who lived on ranches. He also told me that by the time he was seven or eight years old, he was expected to be a top hand around the place.

"It was a matter of economics," he said, leaning on the handle of the shovel. "If I could do the work of a full-grown man, Dad didn't have to hire another one."

He also talked of how he would sit on the fence and watch Tom train horses for hours on end, much to the dismay of his father who thought he should be doing his chores.

"He was amazing to watch," the old man commented. "He could take the wildest, bronkiest son-of-a-gun on the place and have him following him around like a puppy dog in just a few minutes. In a couple of hours, he'd be up on him bareback, ridin' him around with only a rope around the horse's neck to control him. The horse'd never buck or nothin'," he paused, shaking his head. "He was really somethin'."

It was strange hearing the old man talk that way about Tom because I'd seen him do the very same things with horses. I personally felt the same way—that the things he was doing were truly amazing. It never dawned on me that he may have actually learned them from someone and that he felt the same way about that person as I did about him. It was very strange.

At any rate, he went on to tell me that he'd trained his first horse, start to finish, when he was eleven or twelve years old. By the time he was fourteen he was starting fifteen to twenty colts per year.

"Most of those were in the warm months," he said, taking out his pocket knife and digging a small splinter from the palm of his hand that he'd just gotten from the weathered handle of his shovel. "Oh, we started a few in the winter, too, but for the most part, the wind blew too dang hard for us to get anything done."

He also told me that it was around that same time something happened that he'd never forgotten and never would forget. Tom and his father had gone out in the spring, as they did almost every year, to buy or trade for some young horses, which they could train and later sell. This time when they returned, they had a dozen or so head. Almost all of them were very good looking and ranged in age from about two to four. There was one horse in the small herd, however, that stood out from the others. He stood out not because of his striking color or massive physical build, but because the horse was, by far, the ugliest horse he'd ever seen.

"His name was Wil and he was a kind of dirty, grayish-brown kind of color," the old man said, shaking his head as if he still couldn't believe it. "He had a long, long body with little bitty legs, and his head was the size of a fifty-five gallon drum. He had this big Roman nose and these tiny ears that flopped out to the sides when he walked. Most of his mane stuck straight up in the air—the rest of it just went every which-a-way. His tail was this little whisk broom of a thing that was cocked off to the side and almost black, except for a few real long white hairs that hung off the very end." He paused, still shaking his head. "Boy, he was ugly."

"Dad said that the fellow he got him from didn't have the heart to kill him," the old man continued, "but he was so ugly, nobody wanted to buy him either. Dad bought two other horses from him, and just before he paid for 'em, the fellow told him he'd knock two dollars off the price of each one if he'd just take ol' Wil, too." He laughed almost out loud for a few seconds, then said, "Imagine, somebody actually paying you to take a horse. I'd never heard of such a thing. Even a horse as ugly as Wil."

That evening, he continued, after the horses came in, he was sitting on the corral fence watching Wil lumber around, ears flopping, while the three long white hairs of his tail swished feebly at flies. Just then Tom came walking up.

"I remember making a comment," he confessed, "about not understanding why a horse that ugly had been allowed to live as long as he had, which at the time, I guess, had only been about four years.

"Old Tom was leaning on the fence right next to me and, without taking his eyes off the horses, said something that I've never forgot. He said the outside of a horse may be good to look at, but it's what's on the inside that'll tell you if he's good for anything else.

"And you know something," he said, taking the last cigarette from the pack, "old Tom sure knew what he was talking about. I'll be darned if that ugly little horse didn't turn out to be the best one on the place." He lit the cigarette, crumpled up the empty pack, and threw it into the box of his pickup parked nearby. "Oh, we had other good horses. Lots of 'em. But none like him.

"Anything them others could do, ol' Wil could do better. Not only that, but he'd go longer too. Twice as long as any other two put together. I guess it just goes to show ya, you can't judge a book by its cover. Heck, if it'd been up to me, I'd of got rid of him just because he was so ugly. I wouldn't of even given him a chance. It's a good thing Tom knew better." He paused for a second. "I've always kept that in mind over the years."

By this time the trenches that we'd dug were doing the job they were designed to do. There was so much water in the barn, however, that we decided to dig a couple more to help speed up the draining process. While we dug, the old man continued to reminisce.

He said that a few years later his family fell on hard times. One of the horses that they purchased and put in with the herd had evidently been sick with what he called "the fever." As a result, most of their horses, including Wil, became sick and either died or had to be put down. They never recovered financially, and his parents ended up selling the place and moving north to Montana.

"I'm not sure what happened to Tom," he said, with a hint of sadness in his voice. "He must've moved back to the reservation, I guess. Not too many people were willing to give Indians jobs back then."

Not wanting to be a burden to his parents, the old man had struck out on his own after they moved north. He worked at ranch after ranch, trying to improve the training skills that he'd learned from Tom. But at each place, he said, he ran into the same problem.

"All these outfits broke horses pretty much the same way," he told me. "They'd get on and buck 'em till they stopped. That's the way they'd always done it, and none of 'em were too interested in trying something different, especially when a kid was suggesting it. So, I went along with 'em and did things the way they wanted them done."

He stopped briefly to check the water level inside the barn, then continued. "One good thing come out of it, though. I did learn how to ride a buckin' horse. I got pretty good at it too. I just didn't feel right doin' it, knowin' I probably could have got 'em broke without havin' 'em buck."

He told me that even though he was forced to work horses in the way the boss at each different place wanted him to, he was often still able to work on his own training skills. He did this by staying on the ranch on Friday and Saturday nights, when the other hands would go to town.

"I'd kinda make a note in my head," he grinned, "of the horses that the boys were having trouble with. Then on Friday and Saturday nights, when they were in town, I'd work with 'em. Now, I would've got in big trouble if I'd ever been caught, but I never was." He leaned on his shovel, still grinning. "They'd just come back on Monday and their horse's problems would be gone. I don't believe any of them ever figured it out."

It was during that time, when he was traveling from ranch to ranch, that he met a young lady.

"She was the prettiest thing I'd ever seen," he said, as we finished up the last of the two trenches. "She had white teeth and yellow hair. I thought that was really something. With most of the girls I knew, it was the other way around."

Just then the old man looked up at a car that was pulling through the gate. The driver got out and closed the gate behind him before continuing in our direction.

"See who that is, will ya?" he asked, nodding his head toward the car. "I'm gonna check the back of the barn."

Just like that, the stories were over. I couldn't help but feel angry at the driver, even though I didn't know who he was. What I did know was that he was the cause of the interruption that stopped the old man from finishing his stories. As the old man made his way to the back of the barn, I knew that I'd never hear the rest of them. He had never talked like that about himself before, and he never would again. It had been sheer luck that he felt like talking that day. Had it not been for the intruder, I may very well have found out not only what happened to his parents and Tom, but also what became of the yellow-haired girl, how he developed his astonishing horsemanship skills, and most of all, what brought him to own this little hole-in-the-wall horse ranch when he could have easily been paid top money training for some of the biggest horse owners in the country. As it was, though, those questions would never be answered.

The 1956 Chevy that pulled into the yard was in almost as bad a shape as the old man's truck. The only difference was that the car appeared to have a little more paint on it. Other than that, the similarities were amazing.

The car squeaked to a halt about twenty feet from where I was standing, and out of it crawled perhaps the filthiest man I had ever seen. The hair that stuck out from under his dirty, sweat-stained straw cowboy hat was greasy and unkempt. His jeans were so dirty that they actually had a bit of a shine to them, and his boots, with the toes pointing nearly straight up, appeared to be almost completely worn out. He had about four- or five-days' worth of growth on his beard, and he was smoking a cigarette that was about half an inch long.

"Hey, kid," he grunted, while tucking the tails of his brown-and-white checked shirt into his pants. "Who's the ramrod of this outfit?"

"Ramrod?" I asked, never having heard the term before.

"Yeah," he snapped, "the fella that runs this place, where is he?"

"Right here," the old man said, as he emerged from around the side of the barn. "What can I do for you?"

The man stomped out his cigarette and went right over and introduced himself as Burt Nelson, but he said most people who knew him just called him Buzz. He went on to say that he'd been working horses for a place up north until a few days earlier, when he left because of a dispute over his wages. He told the old man that he was looking for a job to tide him over for a while and that he would be more than happy to do anything that needed to be done. He also said he would work cheap, as long as he had a place to stay.

I couldn't believe it. For the third time that day, the old man surprised me. The first time had been that morning when he didn't fire me for leaving the gate open. The second was when he spent the afternoon telling all those wonderful stories, and the third was when, out of the blue, he hired Buzz Nelson.

Now, I don't mind telling you that I had a bad feeling about old Buzz right from the start. Oh, he worked hard all right, and he always did what he was told, but there was just something about him that I couldn't put my finger on. I figured the old man must have felt it too, because over the next couple of weeks, he spent more time with him than anybody else I had ever seen. At first, I thought that he was just kind of keeping an eye on him, you know, making sure he didn't run off with the place. But as time went on, I came to realize that wasn't the case at all. It turned out that what he was doing was showing Buzz how the place ran. He was showing him where everything was and how everything worked. After a couple of weeks, he even began to show him his magical way of working with horses (something I had always thought was reserved just for me). Not only that, but Buzz was soon working several of the horses on the place. Even the horses that I had been riding, horses that were broke and basically just needed exercise.

"Listen, kid," he told me once when the old man wasn't around. "You just run the shovels, I'll run everything else."

By the end of the month, things had gotten so bad that I was seriously considering not going to the old man's place anymore. After all, it certainly appeared that the old man and Buzz had everything pretty well under control. All I was doing at that point was, as Buzz so eloquently put it, running shovels. Surely they could find someone else for that and I could spend the rest of my summer playing ball with my friends.

I had pretty much made up my mind that that's what I was going to do when, one Friday morning, the old man and Buzz came walking up. "I've got some business to take care of out of town," the old man told me, "so I'm going to be gone for a few days. Buzz'll be in charge while I'm gone and I'll need you to be around to give him a hand."

He paused. "Can you do that for me?"

It never failed. The old man's feel and timing were always impeccable in situations like this, just as they were when he was working with horses. Even though he had barely spoken to me in almost three weeks, somehow he knew exactly what was on my mind. I think he knew that I was getting ready to quit and that if he didn't say something, I'd be gone. Even more than that, though, it wasn't what he said that got me to stay, but how he said it. He made it sound like

I wouldn't be there so much to help Buzz, but that by being there I'd be helping him, personally. That was something I couldn't turn down, even if it meant I had to be around Buzz until he got back.

"Sure," I told him. "I can do that."

Later that afternoon the old man jumped in his pickup and headed down the driveway. He hadn't even gotten to the gate before Buzz started in on me.

"You do everything I tell you to do, when I tell you to do it," he grunted, "and we'll get along just fine. If you don't, you'll wish ya had. Understand?"

"Yes, sir," I replied.

"Good," he snapped. "Go make sure them water tanks are full, then go put my saddle away, then go check the back fence line, then come back here and I'll give you somethin' else to do. Got that?"

"Yes, sir."

I could see already that it was going to be one of the longest days of my life. The only saving grace was that I would be done at 4:30 and wouldn't have to be back until 8:00 Monday morning.

Unfortunately for me, the weekend went by way too fast and before I knew it, it was Monday morning. I rode my bike into the yard of the place and, much to my surprise, found that Buzz had done almost nothing all weekend. He hadn't cleaned any of the pens, he hadn't filled any of the water tanks, and I can't prove it, but it looked as though he hadn't even fed. If he did, it wasn't much.

I immediately brought the hose out and began filling water tanks. While they were filling, I went around to each of the pens and fed the horses. Then I began the task of cleaning up two days' worth of manure that had piled up in the pens. It took nearly three hours to get my chores done that morning and at no time did I see hide nor hair of Buzz. Finally, around 11:30, he emerged from the bunkhouse. Well, it wasn't really a bunkhouse. It was just an old chicken coop that the old man had cleaned out, insulated a little, and put a cot in. More than anything, it was just a place for the mice to go to get out of the weather, although I think most of them moved out when Buzz moved in.

Now, Buzz's appearance hadn't varied much during the time that I knew him. He was always dirty and he always smelled bad. However, on this particular day he looked even more gruesome than usual. Apparently he'd been up most of the night seeing how many bottles of cheap whiskey he could drain. By the looks of him, I would've guessed he probably got down quite a few. I had just finished saddling a little palomino mare that I was going to ride when Buzz walked up.

"What do you think you're doing?" he grunted.

"This is the horse I'm supposed to work this week," I replied.

"I'll do all the riding around here," he snapped, as he glared at me through his bloodshot eyes. "You stick to running the shovels. That's the only thing you're good for anyway." With that he grabbed the reins and led the little mare down to the round pen.

Sunny, which was the mare's name, had been a project of mine for about three months. She was very kind, honest, and willing, although not yet trained very well. That was more my fault than it was hers, because I was the one doing the training and at that time my qualifications as a trainer were somewhat less than top notch.

I could see right away that Buzz was going to have trouble with her, or should I say, she was going to have trouble with him. As soon as he got her into the round pen, he pulled her cinch so tight that it appeared she'd have trouble breathing. He threw his leg over her back and dropped his weight into the saddle like he was a sack of potatoes. From forty feet away I could see the whites of Sunny's eyes when he kicked her in the sides to get her to go forward. I don't think she understood why she was being kicked, so as a result she froze in place. This warranted an even harder kick from Buzz, which resulted in the same response from the mare. Five minutes later, still not being able to get her to move, he got off, went to the bunkhouse, put on his spurs, then came back and got back on.

Without hesitation he kicked her hard with his spurs and, much to my surprise and apparently Buzz's too, she came completely untrained. She bucked high and hard for about three jumps before Buzz landed in a heap on the back of his neck, his knees hitting the ground over the top of his head. He rolled over on his side and lay there for a few seconds before getting to his hands and knees. He stayed in that position for a little while, shaking the cobwebs from his head before finally making it to his feet.

He was still a little wobbly, but he did manage, after a time, to catch the mare. He threw himself back in the saddle and kicked her with his spurs. Once again, she dumped him in a heap. This went on for about fifteen minutes before Buzz finally had enough.

After the last time he came off, he jumped to his feet, grabbed the reins, and began jerking on the mare's mouth. He backed her the entire length of the round pen before stopping. He began to kick her soundly in the belly with the toe of his boot. This went on for quite some time, with Buzz cussing the mare as he went, before he finally quit. When he did, he pulled the tack off her and left it in a pile outside the pen. Then, leaving the mare inside the pen, he limped, out of breath, back up to the barn and found me.

I had never in my life seen a person look as bad as he did. Oh, he had looked bad when he crawled out of the bunkhouse that morning, but now, after his little trouble with Sunny, he looked even worse. Both his jeans and his shirt were torn in a couple of places, exposing cuts and bruises on the dirty skin below. There was dried blood on his upper lip that had come from his left nostril, and more blood on his left ear where it looked as though it had been separated from his head. He had a bruise on his chin and one under his right eye, and both elbows and hands were skinned up, as was his right forearm. He was truly a mess.

"I don't want you touching that mare," he snapped, pointing his finger at me with one hand and rubbing dirt from his eye with the back of the other. "You and that old man ruined her by babyin' her the way you do. If I catch you foolin' with her, I'll beat you bloody! You hear me?"

"Yes, sir," I replied.

Then, with as much dignity as he could muster, he turned on his heel and, trying not to limp, made his way back to the bunkhouse and disappeared inside.

I had worked with Sunny for three months and admittedly she wasn't the best-trained horse in the world, but she had sure never acted even remotely close to what she had that day. As I said before, she was quiet and willing and would move forward with just a kiss and a light squeeze of my heels. I certainly never needed to use spurs on her, not that the old man would have allowed me to anyway. I figured that the spurs were probably the reason she blew the way she did, or perhaps it was because she felt the same way about Buzz as I did. At any rate, the damage had been done. Even from a distance, I could see that Sunny was in almost as bad shape as Buzz was. Not only had she worked herself into a lather, she was also bleeding from her mouth and lips, and her legs had several scrapes and cuts where she had clipped herself with her shoes as she scrambled to get away from the beating she had taken.

For the rest of the afternoon Buzz stayed in the bunkhouse, probably recovering from his wounds, and I went about the business of finishing my afternoon chores. Just as I was getting ready to go home, I noticed that Sunny was still in the round pen. Seeing that, I cautiously went up to the bunkhouse and knocked on the door.

"What?" was the explosive response from inside.

"I'm getting ready to leave," I said almost apologetically, afraid of what he might do to me for bothering him. "Do you want me to put Sunny back in her pen? I've already got feed in there."

"No, dang it," he shouted. "I told you to leave her alone and I meant it."

"Yes, sir," I replied, as I scurried off the porch like a kid running from the front door of a haunted house. As quickly as I could, I got on my bike and headed for home.

The next morning I arrived to find everything just the way it had been when I left. Sunny was still in the round pen, the saddle, bridle, and saddle pad were still in a pile outside the pen, and Buzz was still in the bunkhouse. Sunny hadn't had any feed or water in about twenty-four hours. Knowing that, the first thing I did was grab a bucket of water and a couple of flakes of hay and head for the round pen to feed and water her. On my way, I had to walk right past the bunkhouse door. I had no sooner gotten past than Buzz burst through it. He ran up to me, as best he could, and gave me a big shove, knocking me off my feet. As I hit the ground, so did the hay and water, which spilled all over me. Startled and scared, I looked up at Buzz who was standing over me pointing his finger and shouting at the top of his lungs.

"Damn it!" he yelled. "I told you to leave that mare alone and I meant it. She doesn't get any feed or water till I say so! You understand?" Too scared to talk, I could only acknowledge by nodding my head.

"She's gonna learn some respect for me, by God, and if you know what's good for you, you will too!" He was so mad he was actually spitting as he yelled. "Now get out'a here and get some work done. If I catch you even looking at that mare, you'll wish you were never born." He reached out and gave me a hard kick in the leg to get me on my way, which I quickly did.

Sunny received no food or water that day. Not only that, but anytime she would paw in frustration or snake her head through the rails to try to sneak a bite of grass, Buzz, who was sitting nearby, would shoot her with a BB gun. At first he was shooting her in the butt. But as the whiskey he was drinking began to take effect, his aim got worse. Soon he was hitting her in the legs, neck, and sides as well, leaving welts and small puncture wounds.

By late Wednesday afternoon, the next day, Sunny was a pitiful sight. Her coat had lost most of its shine, her flanks were drawn up terribly, and her ribs were starting to show. Her head hung low and she was no longer moving or even attempting to get any of the grass on the outside of the pen. She had so many welts on her from the BBs Buzz had shot at her that it looked like she'd been attacked by a swarm of wasps. To make matters worse, the old man wasn't due back for another two days.

Thursday morning I arrived at work only to find that Sunny was in even worse shape. As I began my morning chores, I started to think of ways to sneak some food and water to the little mare. At the same time I was trying to think of ways to get back at Buzz for what he had done to both her and me.

Just as I finished cleaning my second corral of the day, I heard something that immediately lifted my spirits. It was the distinctive clanging and banging of the old man's truck pulling into the yard. With shovel still in hand, I ran around the corner of the barn and, sure enough, there he was. One day early.

The round pen was close enough to the driveway that, as he came in, there was no way he could have missed seeing Sunny in her diminished state. The look on his face as he walked over to me told me right away that there was going to be trouble because of it.

"What's going on here?" he asked, with a scowl on his face like I'd never seen before.

"Well," I started meekly, "Buzz . . ."

"Buzz did that?" he interrupted.

"He wouldn't let me . . ." but before I could even get the rest out, he grabbed the shovel out of my hand.

"Where is he?"

A glance toward the bunkhouse was all it took. The old man turned and headed that way. He'd gotten almost to the door when Buzz, in unbuttoned jeans, bare feet, and a dirty T-shirt, burst through the door and met him face to face.

A brief but heated conversation ensued, none of which I could hear. However, it was punctuated at the end with Buzz shouting, "You break horses the way you want to, and I'll break 'em the way I want to."

"Not on my place, you don't," the old man replied, with his voice slightly raised. At the same time, though, and with the speed of a flash of light, he whacked Buzz on the right side of his head with the scoop end of the shovel he had taken from me.

Now, the scoop shovel that he used to whack Buzz is commonly referred to as a grain shovel. This particular shovel was not one of the lightweight aluminum shovels that you see today. It was a heavy metal shovel with a solid oak handle. The sound it made when it hit Buzz's head was similar to dropping an iron skillet on a hardwood floor. At any rate, Buzz was on his backside before he knew it.

"You've got five minutes to get your gear packed and get off my place," the old man said flatly. "No one treats my horses the way you did . . . no one."

Buzz, not one to take something like that sitting down, tried to jump to his feet in protest, but was once again met in the head with the business end of the old man's scoop shovel. This one laid him out almost flat and it took him a couple of seconds before he was able to make a third attempt to rise. The final swing of the shovel did lay him out flat. The old man pinned his chest down with the end of the shovel and said something very quietly to him, which I was unable to hear. Whatever he said was apparently enough to get the message across. This time when the old man let him up, Buzz made his way back to the bunkhouse and started packing.

Out of breath, the old man walked back, handed me the shovel and, with a wink and a nod, said, "There, that's the other thing this is used for." After lighting a cigarette, he went to the barn, got a bucket, and filled it half full of water. He took it over and let Sunny drink. When she was done, he told me to do the same thing every fifteen minutes for an hour to help reverse her dehydration before giving her any feed. When she did eat, it should only be a little at a time for the first several hours so that her system could adjust. By doing these things, he said, hopefully she wouldn't get sick on us.

As the old man and I began the task of repairing the damage done to the mare, Buzz quickly headed his car down the driveway and out the gate, never to be seen or heard from again. I don't think I've ever been happier to see a person leave in all my life.

Later that afternoon I noticed the old man over in the round pen putting a halter on Sunny, so I walked down to see what he was doing.

"I think she can go back in her pen now," he told me, as he led her through the gate. "She's doing a lot better."

She definitely was doing better. The difference just a few hours made was amazing. She was very alert, her flanks weren't quite so drawn up, and many of the BB welts had all but disappeared.

"Buzz didn't like you very much, did he?" the old man asked, as we walked Sunny back toward the barn.

"No, he didn't," I replied. "I didn't like him much either."

"I guess not," he nodded. "He was a hard man."

"I know. How come you hired him anyway?"

"Remember a while ago," he began, after giving the question a little thought, "when I told you about Wil, the ugly horse that my dad brought home?" I nodded my head.

"Well," he continued, "nobody wanted to give that horse a chance because he looked so bad. But Tom knew that there may have been a good horse inside that ugly coat of hair. As it turned out, he was right. If we wouldn't have given him a chance, nobody would have ever known that."

I was a little confused. What did this have to do with Buzz? Evidently, the old man could see my confusion, so he went on.

"You can't judge a book by its cover," he said. "It's just like old Wil, but with people, sometimes all people need is a chance. Especially when they're down on their luck. You never know what you might end up with. For all we knew, Buzz could have been one of the best horsemen in the world going through some hard times."

"Yeah, I suppose," I told him. "But he wasn't. He was a drunk."

The old man smiled and shrugged his shoulders. "It doesn't work all the time."

We reached Sunny's pen. The old man pulled her halter off and closed the gate behind her. She went over and began working on the hay that was in her feeder.

"Give her a few days before you start working her again," he said, as we turned and walked back toward the tack room. "By then she should be back to her old self." He didn't say another word until we got inside the tack room door.

"Do you understand why I hired Buzz?"

"I guess so," I told him. "But I don't think I would have hired him. I don't think I'd ever hire someone that looks like him."

"Looks aren't everything," he said, as he hung up the halter. "But maybe you're right. Maybe I shouldn't hire anyone that looks like that anymore. While we're at it," there was a hint of sarcasm in his voice, "I never thought kids were much good for anything neither, so I won't hire any more of them. Would that be okay with you?"

I nodded my approval as he turned, walked out the door, and headed to the hay barn. It took me a few seconds, but the gist of what he said suddenly sunk in. If he'd had that kind of attitude a couple of years earlier, he would never have hired me. As it was, though, he had hired me on the spot, much the way he had Buzz. No questions asked. He had given me, a ten-year-old kid at the time, a chance. As I stepped out the tack room door and looked around, it dawned on me that just about every living thing on the place was there because he'd decided to give it a chance.

There were several cats around the place that he'd found in a sack on the side of the road. They were just babies at the time, but he took them in. His dog slept peacefully in the box of his truck all day long. It was a mutt that he'd found about ten years earlier, after it had been hit by a car and lost a leg. There was a Shetland pony named Shaggy that he had picked up for ten dollars after its previous owners deemed it too dangerous to be around. As it turned out, he was one of the kindest ponies I had ever seen. And then there were the horses, all of them with a history of problems and owners who gave up on them. That is, until they came to the old man. In each case, no matter what kind of problem they had, he had given them a chance to do the right thing. More than that, in each case, he had found a way to help them do the right thing. Ninety-five percent of the horses on the place would surely have been sent to the killers had it not been for him giving them one more chance.

For years, it turns out, he had been going about the business of helping just about everything and everybody he came in contact with, including me. Heck, when I had approached him that summer day two years earlier, I was just a skinny kid who didn't even know which end of the horse to feed. It would have been easy for him to send me away and not be bothered with me. But he didn't. He took me under his wing and showed me the business, literally from the ground up. He showed me everything from how to scoop poop and hammer nails, to how to put a bridle on a horse and sit in a saddle. Even more important than that, though, he showed me what the horse's view of the world is and what I could do to fit into it. He also took the time to show me the things that horses do to communicate, the same things that Tom had taken the time to show him and which are often overlooked—little things like the flick of a tail, the blink of an eye, or the turning of an ear.

He taught me the difference between a horse that was scared, one that was mad, and one that was somewhere in between. He showed me how to teach the ones that have trouble learning, learn from the ones that are trying to teach, and help the ones that want to be helped. He taught me that the best horses aren't always the biggest, the prettiest, or the shiniest. Sometimes they're the little skinny ones with the broom tails and big ears that stand in the back of the pen. Sometimes they're the ones that nobody wants to work with because they're too ugly, too short, or not short enough.

He taught me that good horses, like good people, come in all shapes, sizes, and colors. The only way you'll ever find out if one is any good or not is to give it a chance. Give the horse all the tools, knowledge, and help that he'll need to do a good job and then get out of his way and let him do it. The good horses will work, the others won't. The old man taught me these things not by setting me down and telling me, but by showing them to me in what he did and how he did it. He would buy the jumpy horse with the soft eye, or the old mare that had never been ridden, or the young colt that no one could catch. He'd bring them home and give them a chance. If they worked out, which they did most of the time, fine. If not, they were no worse off than when he found them. The main thing was, at least they had an opportunity.

I picked up many things from the old man in the short time that I spent with him all those years ago. None has had more of an impact on me than the fact that someone of his background, knowledge, and talent would give every horse or person that he came in contact with the same breaks, whether it was a one-eyed horse or a fellow like Buzz who was down on his luck. In his mind, they both deserved an opportunity to make something of themselves. And he was never afraid to help either one.

Over the years, I've found that idea to be the single most important one when it comes to working with horses or working in the horse industry in general. This is especially true in today's world of disposable this and throwaway that. It seems that if the thing we're working with isn't functioning properly, whether it be a horse or a toaster oven, our first inclination is to get rid of it and get one that will work.

That may be fine for the toaster oven, but when it comes to horses, sometimes one more chance is all they need, to show us just how good they really are. If we aren't willing to give them that chance, we'll never know what we might have had.

2

What Makes 'em That Way

MAJOR WAS A three-year-old gelding that I'd been riding for the old man for about a month and a half, and even though he was still in the early stages of his training, I had total confidence that he'd be all right if I rode him away from the barn. With the old man's permission, I mounted up and headed through the gate and onto the trail. As I did, I couldn't help but think about what a great day it was for a ride. It was late June, not too hot and just the hint of a breeze. Originally, I'd planned on working Major for an hour or two. Unfortunately for me, those plans changed about twenty minutes into the ride.

We were a little over a mile away from the barn when the first sign of trouble arose. That trouble, oddly enough, came in the form of a cottontail rabbit that was sitting in plain sight on the side of the trail. It was hunkered down in the short grass having an afternoon snack when we happened upon it. I assumed that because Major's head was turned in the rabbit's direction, he too had seen it. I soon found out, however, that my assumption was more than just a little bit wrong.

As we neared the rabbit, it suddenly moved. Now this was not a big move on the rabbit's part. In fact, the rabbit didn't even appear scared or startled by us. It seemed to be moving just because it had eaten all the grass close by. In order to get anything else to eat, it had to move. That move was nothing more than a lazy, four-inch hop, straight forward. This, apparently, was the first time that Major actually noticed the rabbit, and he definitely did not like what he saw. He snorted and jumped sideways off the trail about three feet. That was enough to start a very interesting chain of events.

By jumping off the trail, Major frightened the rabbit, which quickly decided that perhaps it was time to leave. With that, it scurried off through the grass and into the bushes. That, in turn, unnerved Major, and he spun and began running across the field for all he was worth. I tried pulling back on the reins to slow him down, but that only seemed to make him want to run faster. Before I knew it, we had covered a couple hundred yards and were heading for a small grove of apple trees. I tried to pull his head off to the side in order to turn him away from the trees, but to no avail. We crashed through the trees at top speed, where I broke off branches with my shoulders and head, sending apples in every direction. I bent down over Major's neck in an attempt to limit the surface area I was using for this inadvertent tree trimming, only to find that Major was not real fond of my being in that position. He ducked and turned to the left, just about sending me to the ground, and suddenly found himself face to face with the biggest tree in the grove. Not wanting to hurt himself, I guess, by running into the tree, he ducked back to the right. Luckily, that was enough to throw me back up in the saddle so I could continue the ride. We flew past a few more trees before finally returning to the open, which only served to speed our pace even more.

We covered another thirty or so yards before coming to a gully that ran through the area. The gully was about twenty-five feet wide, with sandy sides that sloped gradually downward. A stream about eight feet wide and three inches deep flowed through it. We came upon the gully so quickly that Major had no opportunity to stop or turn and, as a result, we flew down the bank and skidded right into the water. This was the very first time that Major had been in the water with someone on his back, and he liked it even less than he liked the sight of a rabbit scurrying across the ground. The thing that seemed to bother him the most about being in the water was that every time he put a foot down, he'd splash himself. In an attempt to avoid splashing himself, he began a kind of rearing-lunging motion. That quickly turned into a hopping motion, which consisted of him standing in one place and jumping up and down like a kangaroo. Getting no satisfaction from that activity, he spun and scrambled out of the water and back up the bank in the same direction that we'd just come.

Having lost none of his energy, we raced back through the grove of apple trees, again pruning the trees as we went, and emerged on the other side. We were covering the ground back to the barn rather quickly now, while dodging bushes and rocks and jumping over ditches, and I soon noticed the closed gate, which we'd originally passed through to get on the trail, fast approaching. That made me a little nervous because Major appeared to have no desire to stop for it. My only hope for avoiding a head-on collision with the heavy wooden gate was either to get him stopped before we got to it, which appeared to be completely out of the question, or to turn him away from it before we got there. Having weighed my options carefully, I chose the latter.

We were about fifty feet from the gate and closing fast when I decided to make my move. He was traveling in his right lead, so I thought it best to try to turn him in that direction. I began pulling on the right rein in an attempt to get his head around, and while that did slow him down some, it still didn't turn him. We were just a few feet away from the gate when it dawned on me that perhaps it was time to get off. I figured if he wanted to get hurt by trying to become a permanent fixture of the gate, that was fine with me. It was certainly not something that was high on my list of things to do that day, and I began to make my plans for departure.

I was still holding on to the right rein and just about ready to jump, when he finally decided to do what I was asking him to do—turn. That was the good news. The bad news was that he didn't turn to the right as I'd planned, but instead he went left. That caught me completely off balance and easily dislodged me from the saddle. I did a fancy little somersault as I came off and landed squarely on my backside. My momentum caused me to do a butt-skip across the ground before crashing soundly into the gate. Major turned and ran several yards along the fence line before he finally came to a stop, covered in sweat and breathing hard.

After sitting for a short time to make sure I hadn't broken or twisted anything on either the gate or myself, I slowly got to my feet and made my way over to Major. Understandably, he wasn't real sure that he wanted to be caught again, especially if I was going to get on and put him through another ordeal like he'd just been through. It was for that reason, I think, that he moved away from me the first few times that I tried to catch him. It took three or four attempts, but he finally did stand still long enough to let me approach. I'm quite confident the only reason he let me get so close so fast was that he was simply too tired to run away. Had he any energy left at all, I'm sure he would have used it to run off.

I knew I couldn't let our session end like that, and that once I caught him, I'd have to get back on and ride. But I also knew that he'd been a little traumatized by what had just happened and that if I did ride him, it should be more of a token gesture than anything else. I needed to ask him to do something simple, something that he could perform easily and that wouldn't traumatize him any more. With that in mind, I slowly got back on and gently patted him on his neck. I gave him a little light leg pressure to urge him forward. This was something we'd done a hundred times and, in fact, was one of the very first things he'd learned during his training. His response was automatic. He dropped his head and began walking forward without hesitation. I could feel that he was still somewhat tense, but because he had tired himself out by running all over the countryside, I was pretty sure we weren't going to have a repeat of the stampede that we'd just been through.

We went slowly toward the gate, then turned and walked several yards up the trail before stopping. I dismounted, loosened his cinch, and walked him over to the arena. I led him around the inside of the arena several times to cool him down before finally taking him back to the barn. I figured that was probably enough for one day. I had no sooner tied Major to the hitch rail than the old man emerged from inside the barn. He took one look at the horse, then one look at me, and a big smile crossed his face.

"Have a good ride?" he asked, with just the hint of a chuckle in his voice.

"I've had better," I replied.

"Is that right?" he asked, as he slowly nodded his head. "What happened?"

"He spooked at a rabbit and run off with me."

"Spooked, huh?" He was still nodding his head. "Well, that happens sometimes."

"I don't know why he spooked though," I told him, as I threw the stirrup over the seat of the saddle. "He was looking right at the dang thing when it moved. It wasn't like it took him by surprise or anything, and it only moved about this far." I held up my hands with a four-inch gap between them.

"He probably just didn't see it," the old man said.

"No," I argued. "I'm sure he saw it. He was looking right at it."

"He may have been looking at it," the old man pointed out, "but I doubt that he saw it."

"How can he look at something but not see it?" I asked, almost sarcastically.

"Because," he said, while patting Major on the butt, "horses' eyes don't work the same way ours do."

He was still about half smiling, so it was difficult for me to know if he was telling me the truth or pulling my leg. If I would have had to guess, however, I would have guessed he was pulling my leg. After all, how could it be possible that a horse's eyes, or any other animal's for that matter, don't work the same way ours do? What other way was there?

The old man turned and went into the barn, but quickly returned carrying a bucket and a yellow nylon rope. While I continued to pull Major's tack off, the old man tied one end of the rope to the handle of the bucket.

"Here," he said, placing the bucket on the ground about two feet from Major's left front leg. "I'll show you what I mean."

Leaving the bucket, he turned and began to walk away, stopping only when he reached the other end of the yellow rope, which he was still holding.

"Now," he said, as he draped the end of the rope over his arm, reached in his shirt pocket, and pulled out his cigarettes, "he watched me bring that bucket out of the barn and set it next to him." He took a cigarette from the pack, put it in his mouth, and lit it. "It doesn't seem to bother him much, does it?"

"No, but . . ."

He held up a finger as he took the first drag, basically telling me that he was doing the talking, and the question didn't really need an answer anyway.

"The bucket is in plain sight." Bluish smoke rolled out of his mouth. "The rope that's tied to it is real easy to see, and he can see that I'm holding on to this end of it." He took the end of the rope in his hand once again and bounced it lightly in his palm, as if to check its weight.

"There is absolutely no reason for him to be scared of that bucket, yet if I do this . . ." He very slowly took the slack out of the rope until the bucket tipped, ever so slightly.

The reaction from Major was immediate. His body tensed, his head cocked, apparently focusing his left eye on the bucket, and he quickly stepped sideways, moving his entire body away from it at once.

The old man waited for a second, then gently let the bucket back down to its original position. Major faced the bucket, as best as he could, and with ears up, eyes wide open, and neck arched, he let out a heartfelt snort as if to warn the bucket not to do that anymore.

"Is that how he acted when he saw the rabbit?" he asked, knowingly.

"Kind of," I replied.

"Why do you suppose that is?" He slowly began coiling up the rope and walked back to the bucket. "He saw it, didn't he? Why should something so insignificant scare him like that?"

"I have no idea," I said, bluntly. "It doesn't make any sense."

"Not to you, maybe," he said, with a smile. "But what about the horse? Does it make sense to the horse to be that way?"

"I don't know," I said, without even giving the question much thought. "I guess so, otherwise he wouldn't do it."

"That's right." He bent down and picked up the bucket. "It does make sense to him. But why? What makes 'em that way?"

Frankly, I was in no mood for Twenty Questions and as we made our way back to the barn, my only response to the last one was a shrug of my shoulders. After all, if he was trying to make a point, I wished that he'd just go ahead and make it, instead of making me figure it out for myself, which is what he usually did.

"Horses aren't like us," he continued. "They're different in a whole lot of ways." He took the rope off the bucket handle and put the bucket inside another one that was sitting on the floor. He hung the rope on a nail that was sticking out of the wall near the door.

"The biggest difference, though, is the fact that we humans, as a species, are predators. We hunt for our food, or at least we did. That's why we have our eyes right here in the front of our heads." He took his finger and pointed to his eyes. "We're just like every other predator in that regard. Wolves, lions, bears, dogs, cats, even the birds that hunt other animals, like hawks and eagles, all have their eyes in the front of their heads. Now, the reason for this is so that when we're hunting, we can focus better on our prey."

We made our way back outside where Major was standing. I untied him and began leading him back to his pen. "Horses, on the other hand," the old man continued, "have their eyes on the sides of their head, just like other prey animals, like deer, elk, buffalo, sheep, cattle, even mice and birds. With their eyes on the side of their head, they have a bigger field of vision, which makes it easier for them to see us predators trying to sneak up on 'em."

"If that's the case," I questioned, as I put Major in his pen and pulled his halter off, "why does something as small as a rabbit moving, or that bucket tipping, scare them like it does?"

"Good question," he said, as he leaned against the fence and propped his foot on the bottom rail. "Well, like I said before, horses' eyes don't work the same way ours do. Their eyes are more sensitive to movement than ours are, and they have a hard time distinguishing one object from another. So, when you look at the ground and see a rabbit sitting there, the horse may look at it and think it's a rock. If all of a sudden that rock moves, well, how would you feel?"

"So," I asked, after giving the subject a little thought, "what you're saying is that it wasn't so much the rabbit that scared Major, but what the rabbit did?"

"It sure would appear that way," he said, with a grin.

"And that's why you said he didn't see it, even though he was looking right at it."

"Could be," he smiled.

He went on to explain that the horse's biggest asset in his fight for survival in the wild is his ability to outrun all his predators. It's his eyesight that often gives him the crucial edge that he needs so desperately to accomplish that. Because his eyesight is designed to help him react to the movement of an object instead of first distinguishing what the object is, he is often able to outdistance his predators before they can even get close to him. There will always be time later to see what was causing the movement, which is exactly what he'll do once he feels he's put a safe enough distance between it and himself.

The old man also explained that the reason Major didn't respond to me after he started to run off was because when something scares a horse that bad, he believes he is running for his life. Once a horse begins to run for his life, nothing else is important to him. A horse's common sense and ability to reason go right out the window and instincts take over. His main concern is to get as far away from whatever frightened him as possible, and nothing else matters. The horse completely forgets where he is, what he was doing, and where he was going. The fact that someone is on his back means nothing to him at all. In some cases, having someone on his back may actually frighten him even more. After all, if a predator is after him, that's where it will attack to try to bring him down. At that point, stopping is not an option.

Major's reaction to the rabbit began making sense to me. His response was a simple case of "better safe than sorry." Get away from it first, then worry about what it is later. What didn't make sense to me, however, was why he acted so scared when the old man moved that bucket. After all, Major watched him bring the bucket out of the barn, tie the rope to it, walk away, then pull on the rope, which tipped the bucket. Common sense would say that, even if his eyes didn't work the same way as ours, he must have seen and understood what was happening. He must have known that the old man was causing the bucket to move. But if he did, why did it scare him? And if he didn't, why didn't it scare him more?

As the old man and I made our way back up toward the barn, I asked him those very questions. Unfortunately for me, the answer he gave wasn't much help. He told me simply to "think about it." This meant that if it was really that important to me to know the answer, I should figure it out for myself. I hated it when he did that. It was obvious that there was a reason for the old man's demonstration and that the reason was important. The question then was how important it was to me to know what the reason was.

I knew that he brought that bucket out to make a point and that part of what he was trying to say was that horses don't see the same way we do. Okay, that part I got. But there was more to it. There had to be. That demonstration was way too elaborate just to tell me that horses' eyes don't work like ours do. The frustrating thing was that for the life of me, I couldn't figure out what it was he was trying to say, and he was not about to tell me.

The answer finally came to me years later, but it did so in a rather unusual way. I was behind the chutes at a rodeo, talking to a friend of mine, when it happened. We were looking out toward the area where the ropers were getting their horses ready for the competition, when unexpectedly a burst of wind came up. The wind took a saddle blanket that was draped over the tailgate of one of the pickups and literally threw it at a horse that was tied to a nearby trailer. From where we were standing, it appeared as though the blanket jumped off the truck and attacked the horse all by itself. The horse must have gotten the same impression because that blanket scared him half to death. He pulled back hard, breaking his lead rope, and took off running for all he was worth. Now this was a seasoned roping horse that had been everywhere and seen everything. Everything, that is, except a blanket jumping off a truck and attacking him. That blanket, in the horse's mind, was doing something that it wasn't supposed to do. It was moving all by itself.

It dawned on me that maybe Major became scared when the old man tipped that bucket for the same reason. He was scared, not because of what the old man was doing, but because of what the bucket was doing. It was doing something that it didn't normally do unless a person was holding on to the handle. The fact the somebody was making the bucket move from twenty feet away was something Major had never seen before, and so it was hard for him to comprehend. Just like the wind moving that blanket. We know the wind is moving it, because we know the physics behind it. Horses, on the other hand, are not very good at physics and so they take things a little more literally.

What Major saw was the bucket, a familiar object, doing a very unfamiliar thing—moving without a person touching it. Major had seen buckets before, lots of them. They were certainly nothing new. He had seen buckets being carried from one place to another, he had seen them being picked up and put down, he had walked past them as they sat motionless on the ground, and he had even drunk water and eaten grain out of them. The one thing he had never seen a bucket do, however, was move without a person being attached to it and to him that was simply unacceptable behavior on the bucket's part.

After all those years, what the old man had been trying to say finally dawned on me. He'd been saying that horses not only don't physically see things the way we do, but they also see things different mentally. When we see a large dark rock on the side of the trail, the horse might see a bear lying in wait. He might see a small stream as moving ground, and a paper sack blowing down the road as an unidentified running object. These are all things that we, as humans, take for granted. The horse, on the other hand, sees them as potentially life-threatening predators that he has no business being around, and he cannot understand why we want him to be near them. The more we fight with him to force him through, over, or near unfamiliar things or situations, the more he'll fight with us to stay away from them. It's simply the horse's way of telling us that this doesn't look right to him, and until we can prove that it isn't going to hurt him, he'll just stay at a safe distance, thank you very much.

It was this realization about horses that helped me to look at them in a whole new light. Before, I think I considered them as being nothing more than large dogs that thought like people. Now I know better. Now I know that their entire make-up is designed for one purpose and one purpose only—survival. Theirs, not ours. One good look at the horse, as an animal, will confirm that statement.

It's easy to see, just by looking, that the horse is designed for speed. He has long, thin legs under a large, muscular body. The thin legs make for easier and quicker movement in case a fast getaway is needed. Large, heavy legs would be too cumbersome in the same situation and would also require a much larger body to power them, causing a tremendous loss of speed and more vulnerability to predators. The large, powerful body that the horse does possess helps to ensure that, even if a predator should catch him, the horse would still be difficult to bring down. In addition, nature has provided the horse with some very acute senses to help him avoid being caught in the first place. His eyesight is a primary one, and the placement of his eyes in his head helps to ensure that they can be used at all times. Many people think the horse's eyes are placed where they are because that's where they look the best. Well, I agree with that, but it isn't really the reason. A horse's eyes are where they are so that he can be eating in relatively tall grass and still see his surroundings. With his nose down, he can still see above the top of the grass.

The horse also has a highly developed sense of hearing, which he uses in tandem with his sight. Many times he will hear something that doesn't sound right to him long before he sees what it is, although the sound of something strange will seldom send him stampeding off like the sight of something strange will. When he does hear something that doesn't sound right to him, he will first stop whatever he's doing, then raise his head and stare in the direction of the sound. If whatever made the sound doesn't look right either, chances are he probably won't wait around to see if it's hungry.

And then there is the one sense that the horse uses probably even more than his sight and hearing, and is the one that we overlook the most. That is, his sense of smell.

Like so many other horse people, I have seen horses that, after being moved from one location to another, will refuse to drink because the water at the new place smells different from what they are used to. They may also refuse to eat because the feed smells different. I've seen horses on the trail suddenly lock up and refuse to go any farther because they've picked up an unfamiliar odor, and horses that refuse to load into a brand-new trailer because of the strong smell of new paint and rubber.

I even recall one time I was called to a place to evaluate a horse that the owners were getting ready to sell. They wanted to know what he'd be worth so they'd be sure to get a fair price for him. The woman who called told me a little bit about the horse over the phone. She said that they'd owned him for about three years and that he was a great trail horse. She also said that he loaded well in trailers, was easy to shoe, and was bombproof, meaning, of course, that almost nothing frightened him.

"He does have one small problem," she said, rather sheepishly. "He seems to hate women."

"Hate women?" I asked. "Has he always been that way?"

"I don't think so," she replied. "He's just kind of gotten that way over the last year or so."

I remember thinking that that didn't sound good. There's always a reason for a horse to act badly toward one type of person or another, and it was usually the person's fault. At any rate, I agreed to have a look at the horse.

The place was in a rather new subdivision, tucked back in a heavily wooded area. I couldn't help but think to myself as I pulled through the gate that the folks who owned it must have been pretty well off. Sitting in front of what appeared to be a half-million-dollar home was a brand-new dually pickup. Beside it was a smaller pickup that appeared to be just as new, and in one of the four garages that sat open was one of those newfangled sports cars with the name that no one can pronounce. In one of the other garages sat a red Cadillac convertible. On the side of the house was a new six-horse gooseneck trailer, and next to that was a thirty-foot motor home with a Jeep attached to the back bumper by a tow bar.

I climbed out of my old pickup and made my way up to the door, found the doorbell, and pushed it. The doorbell sounded like the chimes you hear in one of those great big churches, and I was sure anyone within a four-mile radius now knew that somebody was at the door. I can't tell you how surprised I was when a fellow in a faded flannel shirt, blue jeans, and cowboy boots answered the door.

He introduced himself as Art Calender and said that his wife, Jennie, who was the one who'd called me, would be right out. In the meantime, we could go on down and have a look at the horse. We made our way to the back of the house and down a hill on a blacktopped path to a large barn that was nicer than most of the houses I've lived in. Standing in a spotless corral were five of the nicest-looking horses I'd ever seen. As we entered the corral, Mr. Calender began telling me the names and lineages of each of the horses, until we finally came upon the one I'd come to see. He was a big bay gelding named Whisper who was standing by himself in a pen on the side of the barn. We walked over to the pen to get a closer look and almost immediately we were approached by the horse. He seemed very friendly, and as Mr. Calender began rattling off his list of attributes and accomplishments, I had a hard time believing that anyone would have trouble handling or riding him.

We climbed in the pen with him and Mr. Calender went around and picked up each of his feet to show me how well he did that. He jumped on the horse bareback, without so much as a lead rope around his neck to control him. He rode him around the inside of the pen, using only leg cues to turn and stop him, then jumped off and walked back to where I was standing. Whisper followed quietly behind.

"He's a great horse," he said, patting him softly on the shoulder. "I'd love to keep him and sure would if it wasn't for the fact that he hates women."

"Boy," I said, shaking my head. "It's hard to believe that this horse could hate anyone."

"I know." He shrugged his shoulders. "But he sure does. You'll see here in a minute, as soon as my wife gets down here."

There was a slight breeze blowing from the direction of the house, and he had no sooner finished speaking than I began to notice a real interesting odor. I think the horse noticed it too, because he began to fidget. He shook his head a couple of times, pawed at the ground, snorted, then turned and trotted over to the other side of the corral where he continued to shake his head and snort. I noticed that the other horses began to snort as well, although not nearly as much nor nearly as long.

A short time later, Mrs. Calender appeared on the path leading from the house to the barn. She was a very attractive lady in her mid to late forties, wearing a bright pink blouse, designer blue jeans, three-hundred-dollar cowboy boots, and perhaps ten thousand dollars worth of jewelry. I noticed that, as she got closer, the odor was getting stronger, and Whisper seemed to be getting more and more agitated.

She walked through the gate and, like a mother greeting her young children, called each of the horses by name while she patted and rubbed their heads. She then turned and, with a bounce in her step, made her way over to us. Mr. Calender met her at the fence where she reached over and gave him a kiss square on the lips, before finally turning and introducing herself to me. It was easy to tell where the odor that I'd been smelling was coming from. It was coming from her. Now, don't get me wrong, this was certainly not the odor of someone who hadn't bathed in a year or two, although I'm not so sure that wouldn't have been somewhat of an improvement. Instead, it was the smell of a very expensive perfume, one that, had it been used with a little restraint, would probably smell quite good. Unfortunately, that was not the case here. She smelled as if someone had sprayed it on her with a fire hose. She had so much of it on that to be right up close to her literally hurt my nose in that little area up inside my head, right between my eyes. The strength of it even caused me to sneeze a time or two, which caused both of them to say "God bless you" about the same time I apologized for sneezing.

"Well," she asked, as she leaned on the fence and looked over at the horse who was, by now, pitching a pretty good fit on the other side of the pen, "what do think of ol' Whisper?"

"Pretty nice horse," I commented, trying real hard to talk without actually inhaling.

"He sure is," she smiled. "I just wish he didn't hate me so. Artie gets along with him just fine, but he does this every time I come around. He'll even act this way if Artie is riding him and I'm on another horse. I guess it's just one of those personality things." She paused, glancing at her husband who was kind of staring at the ground. "We hate to get rid of him," she continued, "but he's just no good to us if he's going to be this way."

"I sure agree with that," I told her, as I tried to move, undetected, to a comfortable place upwind. "But the reaction he has to you might not be a personality thing."

"Really?" she asked, moving her left foot to the bottom rail of the fence. "What other explanation could there be?"

"Well," I said, as I moved around to the side of the pen, acting as though I was trying to get a better look at the horse's conformation, "I noticed that you seem to be wearing a little perfume."

"Perfume?" she questioned. "Well, yes, I did put a little on before I came out. But surely that wouldn't cause this kind of behavior, would it?"

"Well, actually," I said, trying to be as diplomatic as possible, "sometimes it does."

I went on to explain that horses have a very highly developed sense of smell and something like perfume can be very irritating to them. One way to find out if that was the case here, I suggested, would be to put a small amount of mentholated rub around each nostril—the horse's, not ours—then see if he still reacted the same way when she came around. The rub would mask the smell of the perfume, which would tell us if the horse was responding to the person or the perfume.

"I guess it's worth a try," she said, looking at her husband. "What do you think, honey?"

"Sure," he shrugged his shoulders. "I'd hate to get rid of him if we don't have to."

"Okay," she smiled. "I'll run up and see what I can find. I'm sure we've got something that will work."

She went up to the house and returned a short time later with a small blue jar filled with Vicks VapoRub. Mr. Calender went into the barn and brought back a halter that he put on the horse. I took the jar and applied the Vicks lightly on Whisper's nose. Then we went up to the house and waited for about half an hour while Whisper got used to the smell. When we returned, he was standing quietly in the middle of the pen and was showing no sign of discomfort at Mrs. Calender's presence or from the Vicks on his nose. In fact, for the first time in almost a year, she was actually able to go in the pen and pet him.

"Isn't that something?" she marveled, as she stroked his neck. "I never even considered that something I was wearing was causing the problem. I always thought it was just that he didn't like me." She kissed the horse's neck and spoke to him. "Well, I guess we know what to do now. We'll just have Artie come down and put this stuff on your nose before I come see you."

"That's one option, I guess," I told her. "Another one might be to not wear any perfume when you're around him. Putting that stuff on his nose all the time could really irritate it."

"I suppose that's true," she said, with a big smile. "I guess I'm just not thinking today."

Half an hour later I was on my way home thinking of how true that statement was. Not just for Mrs. Calender, but for all of us who own or work with horses. How many times have we done things to our horses without even considering what kind of effect we might be having on them? Things that, because of the type of animal horses are, may bother them to the point that they become irritable, frightened, belligerent, or hard to handle. Then, because we don't really understand the horse as an animal, we think that the only way to correct the problem is by force or physical discipline, which usually only serves to make matters worse.

For example, some time ago I was visiting with a friend at the stable where she boarded her horse. I'd just arrived when the owner of the place brought out a horse that he'd bought at a sale only two days before. The sale had been seven or eight hundred miles away in South Dakota, and this particular horse had been taken to the sale from Minnesota, another four or five hundred miles from there. As soon as the fellow had gotten the horse home from the sale, he took him from the trailer and put him directly into a box stall, where the horse had been standing ever since. Now, two days later, he was taking him out of the stall to see what kind of horse he was.

He put the horse in cross ties and thoroughly brushed him down. Then he brought out a blanket and saddle, which he simply threw up on the horse's back without giving the horse much of a chance to see what he was doing or how he was going to do it. He tightened the cinch about as tight as he possibly could, then went over to his "bit box," a box containing about thirty different bridles with bits, to chose just the right one for this particular horse in this particular situation. He returned with a twisted-wire, half-snaffle, half-curb-bit-looking thing, which he shoved into the horse's mouth. He led the horse outside, where once again he tightened the cinch before jumping into the saddle. As he landed in the saddle, he unknowingly hooked the horse in the side with one of his spurs, which caused the horse to jump and snort. The man would have none of that behavior. In order to reprimand the horse and show him who was boss, he began jerking on the reins while kicking the horse with his spurs. The horse, having no idea what he'd done wrong, quickly spun in a circle. He then leapt forward for several yards, spun another circle and hopped a few times, before finally stopping. His eyes were open so wide with fear that it seemed as though more white was showing than dark, and every muscle in his body was tense and quivering.

"Welcome to your new home," I thought to myself.

Over by the house several dogs were barking and running inside a small pen. Horses ran up to the nearby fence to see what all the commotion was, and several people came out of the barn to see if there was going to be a wreck. In the middle of all that was one young horse that was a long way from anything that looked, sounded, or smelled like anything even remotely familiar to him. The man quickly spurred him forward, riding him down to the arena, where he spooked and jumped at a variety of scary-looking things. At the same time, he was being forced to perform flawless stops, turns, and lead changes, all of which he was having trouble with.

"He might make a good horse," the man said, after about an hour or so of jerking and spurring, "but he sure don't know as much as they said he did."

It was fairly obvious that this fellow had no idea what makes a horse a horse, and he didn't really care. If he had, he would have taken a little more time to listen to what the horse was trying to tell him and then tried to help him through the trouble he was having.

Instead of perhaps giving the horse a day or two to adjust to his surroundings by turning him out in a paddock or corral, the man simply jumped on him as though the horse was nothing more than a motorcycle with hair, and expected him to perform that way. The horse, however, responded more like a horse.

I don't know how many horses I've seen that are in the same boat. They have what I would call a problem owner. That is, an owner who has little comprehension of why horses act and react the way they do and, as a result, inadvertently causes a horse's problem behavior simply by owning it. These owners treat their horses as inanimate objects and tools, rather than living, breathing animals that may have a little different agenda than they do. As owners, when a problem arises between our horse and ourselves, we usually get in such a big hurry to try to "fix" the problem, we don't take the time to find out why the problem exists in the first place. We don't think about the horse.

The horse, on the other hand, is almost always thinking about us. He has no other choice. By some wacky twist of fate, he has been thrust into our world and forced to conform to it. The ones that don't conform have what can only be referred to as a gloomy future.

What most people don't understand, I think, is that once we see the horse's point of view and understand the way horses see the world around them, working with them becomes a whole lot easier. By understanding the horse, we can distinguish between one that is scared, one that is spoiled, and one that simply doesn't know any better. Not only that, but we can then understand how the horse got that way to begin with and how to help it. Then, instead of forcing the horse to fit into our world, we can meet it halfway, which, I would wager to guess, is the only thing a horse would ask of us, if it could.

3

A Good Horse Is Never a Bad Color

IT WAS VERY seldom that the old man took an outside horse in for training. In fact, in the four-and-a-half years I worked with him, I can only recall one. This particular horse had come from somewhere out of state, if I remember correctly, and belonged to the granddaughter of a friend of his. It had evidently been to several other trainers who were unable to get anything done with it, and it had actually become worse with each successive trainer. He agreed to take the horse for the simple reason that a friend had asked him to and because it had been put to him that, if he couldn't do anything with the horse, nobody could. In other words, he was that horse's last chance.

Other than the old man having put on a clean shirt for the occasion, the little gelding arrived quite unceremoniously on a Monday morning in early summer. The truck and trailer that brought him were followed closely behind by a brand-new Olds 88, and as both vehicles pulled to a stop in the yard, the reason for the clean shirt suddenly became apparent. The driver of the car was a very pretty lady, about the same age as the old man, although with considerably less mileage. She was dressed in a blue shirt and brown vest, blue jeans, and cowboy boots. She had long, grayish hair pulled back in a ponytail, and the greenest eyes I think I'd ever seen. The old man pulled off his hat as soon as she opened her door. Taking his hat off always exposed his very prominent receding hairline, made even more prominent by the fact that the top of his head was almost white compared to the dark brown of his face and hands. As the woman walked up and gave him a hug, a young girl about my age emerged from the passenger side of the car. The lady introduced her as her granddaughter, whose name was Donna.

While the two were talking, the driver of the truck came over and asked where he should put the horse. The old man directed him over to an empty pen and he quickly backed his trailer up to it. While the old man opened the door to the trailer, the driver grabbed a long stick that he had in the back of his pickup and began poking at the horse through the vents of the trailer.

"That isn't real necessary, is it?" the old man asked, in a way that sounded more like a statement than a question. The driver didn't answer. He simply spit some tobacco juice on the ground and continued to poke and prod the horse forward. The horse scrambled around in the trailer, falling a couple of times before finally bursting out the trailer door and into the pen. He ran for the far end of the pen, apparently looking for a way out, before stopping dead in his tracks, dropping his head to the ground, and blowing hard through his nose, which kicked up a considerable dust cloud. The old man closed the trailer door while the driver came around and closed the gate to the pen.

"Damn Arabs," the driver said, as he latched the gate. "You could take the whole bunch of 'em, put 'em all together, and you still wouldn't have one that'd be worth a spit."

"That's just the attitude that has got this poor horse in the state he's in," the woman said, with a slight hint of disgust in her voice.

"It's not the attitude," the man said, as he spit on the ground. "It's the horse."

"Yes, well, thank you for your time," the woman retorted, as she reached in her pocket and pulled out a small money clip full of twenty-dollar bills. "I believe we agreed on eighty dollars for your services."

"Yeah, but there have been some other expenses that I wasn't counting on."

The woman simply ignored the statement, peeled four bills out of the clip, and handed them to him.

"The way I got it figured," the man said, as he took the bills, "I'm going to need another forty dollars."

"Well," the woman said, as she returned the clip back to her pocket, "the way I've got it figured, eighty dollars means eighty dollars. If you thought you were going to need more money, you should have told me that before we left." She smiled as she stuck out her hand to shake his. "Again, thank you for your time."

The man stood for a second counting the four bills, not once, but twice, then looked over at the horse.

"This just ain't going to be enough," he grunted. "I guess I'll have to load that horse up and haul him back to where he come from."

"Now, Mr. Harris," the woman smiled, "we both know that you're not going to do that, so why don't you stop all this fussing, take your eighty dollars, and be on your way."

The man's face twisted up into a scowl of frustration and he turned to look at the old man as if trying to muster some support. The old man simply smiled and shrugged his shoulders as if to say, this argument is over and there is nothing either of us can do about it. The fellow looked back at the woman, counted his money one more time, spit, then went back to his truck, got in, and drove away.

"Well," the woman started, acting as though the episode about the money had never happened, "you can see that we have a little problem here. Old Brownie has had a pretty rough go of it over the last few months, and I'm afraid he might be ruined."

She went on to say that the horse had been to three different trainers in the past ten months and that each of the trainers seemed to have less luck with him than the last. He'd gotten to the point that he was difficult to catch and halter, and anything beyond that, such as saddling, bridling, or riding was out of the question. His feet were in terrible shape because no one could get close enough to him to pick a foot up. If someone actually did get close enough to touch one of his legs, he responded by kicking and striking until he'd made it clear that he'd simply rather not have his feet messed with. No one had yet found the right button to push to persuade him otherwise.

"He's definitely going to be a project," the woman said. "I sure hope you can do something with him. This is Donna's very first horse. Or, I should say, the first one she's bought with her own money."

"I'm beginning to think I made a mistake," the little girl added sadly. "Everybody told me not to buy an Arab because they were so stupid. I guess maybe they were right."

"Oh," the old man smiled, "I wouldn't give up on him just yet. We might be able to find a way around him for you."

"I sure hope so," she said. About that time, I happened to glance over and notice the woman giving the old man a wink, as if the two of them knew something that the rest of us didn't. As it turned out, I think maybe they did.

The old man went over and grabbed a couple flakes of hay from a nearby bale. He went inside the pen, placed the hay in the feeder, and fluffed it up as if he were arranging it. Then, before coming out of the pen, he turned and took three steps toward the horse, stopped for just a second, then turned and left the pen.

An hour later the woman and her granddaughter left for home and I went about the business of finishing my morning chores. It took me about forty-five minutes before I got around to the new Arab's pen. Just as I was getting ready to go in and check his water tank, the old man came walking up.

"I'll tell you what," he said, as he approached. "Why don't you let me take care of him for the next few days, at least till he gets used to the place?"

"Sure," I said, happy to have one less horse to look after.

"He sure is a nice-looking horse, isn't he?" the old man said, as he looked over the fence at the dark-brown gelding.

"Yeah," I agreed. "I've always liked the way Arabs look."

It was true. There is just something about the breed that has always caught my eye. I remember, as a small child in school, drawing pictures of horses with dished faces and ears that almost touched at the tips when they stood straight up. I had never had much practical experience with the breed, though, for the simple reason that the old man bought and dealt mostly with quarter horses. As a result, I'd never really been exposed to the myth that the breed was "stupid" until that day. I must say, it would have been very disappointing to me had that particular myth turned out to be true.

"When are you going to get started with him?" I asked, hoping to see what kind of magic he was going to work on the gelding.

A kind of impish grin began to cross his face as if he were planning on doing something sneaky. "I already have," he replied, as he turned and walked away.

That told me that if I wanted to see what he was going to do with this horse and how he was going to do it, I'd better stay on my toes. It was going to be one of those times when, if I blinked, I was going to miss it. And as it turned out, I was right.

The things that he did with the horse in the first week were so small that it was hard to tell that anything was taking place. All he did was go in the pen with some hay, put the hay in the feeder, turn and take three steps toward the horse, then leave. Evidently, this was doing more to help build the horse's confidence than it appeared, because within about a week and a half the old man could walk in the pen and actually go up and pet the horse. Within two weeks he could put a halter on him, and within three weeks, he could go in and put a saddle on him without having to halter or tie him to anything first. After a month and a half, he could get on and ride him in the pen using nothing but a halter to turn and stop him, and within two months, he was riding him out on the trail. By the end of the summer, the horse was crossing water while being ridden, loading into a two-horse trailer by himself, being roped off of, doing flying lead changes, and performing sliding stops and rollbacks. He had also become very easy to catch, groom, and shoe, as well.

The feats that the old man accomplished with the horse in the short time that he had him were, to me, nothing short of amazing. When the horse arrived at the place, it seemed as though everyone had given up on him ever becoming anything more than the waste of a little girl's money. The fact that he was an Arab only seemed to confirm that idea.

The one person who seemed undaunted over the task of turning a seemingly worthless Arab into a "real" horse was the old man. Not only that, but it was almost as if he did what he did to prove a point. That point, I think, was that any horse can be a good horse if you give them the opportunity. Even an Arab.

Unfortunately, I have run into very few people since my time with the old man who shared the view that any horse can be a good horse. Not that those people aren't out there, mind you. It's just that I haven't seen very many of them. Rather, the statements that I hear from people most often are that this is a worthless breed and that is a worthless breed. As if the training and handling that the horses are subjected to throughout their lives have absolutely nothing to do with their dispositions. That, it seems, is seldom taken into consideration by the person making such statements.

The Arabian is a perfect example of a breed of horse that is often misunderstood by the general horse-loving public. It is a breed that is perceived by many as being high-strung, spooky, and hard to handle. They are also perceived as being unaffectionate, hard to train, and unresponsive. Personally, the only time I have found those descriptions to be true is when the horse has had no other alternative—someone has made the horse that way. I think that most people who have trouble with Arabs are people who try to train them without really understanding the breed, or they're people who buy an Arab after it has already developed one or more of the problems that people seem to think they're all born with.

Several years ago I had the opportunity to work with two such horses. They were half brothers. Both geldings were gray, Arab/quarter horse crosses. The older one was twelve, the younger one was ten. Both horses had been owned by a fellow who had raised them since birth and who, in my opinion, is the type of person that gives the Arab breed a bad name because of the way he trained them.

The horses came to me for rehabilitation through a horse rehab center that I work with here in Colorado. They didn't need rehabilitation in the physical sense, like so many of the horses that come to the organization. Rather, they had been abused mentally. When they arrived, they were both wearing halters that had been on them for over eight years. They'd been wearing them for so long that their heads had actually grown around the nose bands, and the halters themselves were faded and frayed. I had to take my knife and cut the halters off their heads because the buckles had rusted in place and were impossible to open. Once I got the halters off, I turned the horses out in a one-acre, square corral, then enlisted the help of my long-time friend and assistant, Susie Heide, for the actual rehab process.

These horses appeared to be in much the same condition as the Arab the old man had worked with all those years ago. They were both terrified of people and anything having to do with them. The younger one was so bad off that any time someone came anywhere near him, he would suddenly and uncontrollably begin to shake. If you walked behind him, he would literally almost sit down, tucking his tail tightly between his legs as if he were certain he was about to be beaten from behind. Because of their fear of people, we decided to use the same type of easy, slow training process that the old man had used on the horse that had been brought to him.

For the first week or so, we did very little with the pair except feed and water them. During the second week, we simply worked on approaching and touching them. By the third week, they had enough confidence in us to allow themselves to be haltered and led out of the corral. It was at this time, however, that we were forced to change strategies with the two.

While the older horse was responding quite well to everything we were doing, the younger of the two was still quite frightened by even the smallest things that we would do with him. Because Susie had grown attached to the younger one, she offered to continue to work with him on the slow and sometimes thankless job of trying to gain his trust, while I proceeded with the other. I should point out that most people would have given up on the young horse at this point, probably blaming his deficiencies on the fact that he was part Arab. Susie, on the other hand, was not one to be put off or give up so easily.

Over the next several months, the older horse progressed in leaps and bounds. Not only were we able to ride him both in the arena and out on the trail, but we were also able to rope off of him and gather horses off of him. Only four months after he'd come to us, we were able to enter him in a couple of classes at a local horse show. He didn't take home any ribbons from the show, but that wasn't the purpose of his attendance anyway. He went for the simple reason that he could. A couple of weeks after the show he was deemed fit for adoption by the rescue organization that owned him and, as a result, soon went to a new home.

A few months later, Susie had the younger horse responding to her in ways that could only have been imagined when he first came to us. Not only was he allowing himself to be saddled, bridled, and ridden, but he was also being taken out on the trail and working off leg cues as well. In fact, when the organization finally deemed the gelding fit for adoption less than a year later, Susie, who had done most of his rehabilitation and by that time had fallen in love with him, was first in line.

The young gelding that was terrified of people and that would shake with fear any time someone came near him, now gives rides to Susie, her husband, their young son, and anyone else who happens to want to go for a ride when they stop by her place. All this from a half-Arabian gelding that most people would have probably given up on just because of his breed.

As far as I was concerned, Susie was the perfect choice to give me a hand with these two geldings because she was not only an excellent hand with horses, but she is also a very big advocate of the Arab breed itself. In fact, if the fellow that had previously owned these horses was the epitome of everything that can be wrong with an Arab trainer, Susie was the epitome of everything that can be right. Her own horse, a petite bay mare named Tadpole, was the type of horse that anybody would love to own. Susie could do anything with her. She had not only won countless ribbons with her at Arabian shows in both western and English pleasure classes, but she had also trained her to be an excellent trail horse as well. Susie had once used her to help drive our herd of thirty or so horses from their winter pasture to the home place some thirty-five miles away with a gain of four thousand feet in elevation. While all the people on the drive that day were well mounted, little Tadpole was the only horse that carried her rider the entire way without so much as taking a deep breath or breaking a sweat. A true testament, I think, to the stamina of the Arab breed. The rest of the horses being ridden that day played out about halfway through and had to be switched.

I had often teased Susie about owning a "foo-foo" horse, referring to the diminutive, almost toy-like stature that Tadpole had. But if the truth be known, I always admired the combination of frail beauty and unyielding toughness that the little mare possessed and the training ability that Susie exhibited by bringing out the best in her.

Over the last several years, I have only been fortunate enough to run across a couple of people with similar training talent. People who not only want to produce a good, well-trained horse, but who also care about each particular horse as an individual, no matter what size, breed, or color the horse happens to be. By working with each horse as an individual, they often sacrifice the speed of the training process for the quality of the finished horse. But to them, it doesn't matter. A good horse with a sound mind, they feel, is better than a mechanical horse with no mind. What I mean by a "mechanical" horse is one that does things because, during his training, he has been forced to do them. He doesn't work because he wants to, he works because he has to. There is no feeling in what he does, just a mechanical motion.

The trainer who works with each horse on an individual basis usually tries to form his or her training methods to fit the horse's personality. By doing that, the trainer is usually able to avoid the mechanical feeling you sometimes get from a horse. In its place is a more natural flow and a genuine willingness from the animal. Put simply, it is like forming a partnership between the horse and rider. A couple of years ago I was able to watch one of these partnerships develop between a young trainer and a horse that nobody wanted.

The trainer's name is Kristie Charles and at the time she was working as the head wrangler for the Wind River Guest Ranch in Estes Park, Colorado. I met Kristie through the owners of the ranch, Rob and Jere Irvin, when they asked if I'd be able to give them a hand purchasing and training some horses to be used in their string. It was during my second year of working for the Irvins that Kristie and I happened across a little horse that we thought, with some work, might fit right into the horse program at the ranch.

The horse was a small, black-and-white paint gelding that had sort of worn out his welcome with the folks who owned him. He'd developed a terrible attitude toward people in general and he had become difficult to ride and handle. He had gotten so bad, in fact, that he'd taken to bucking and rearing a little when things weren't going just the way he thought they should. When he wasn't rearing or bucking, he was acting up in other ways. He was next to impossible to get into a lope, and if he did lope, you couldn't get him to stop. He didn't turn very well in any gait and getting him to back up while riding him was out of the question.

Originally, the little gelding had been purchased for the family's ten-year-old girl to use in 4-H. He was just the right size for her, standing about fourteen hands, and, at first, seemed to have just the right temperament, appearing very quiet and willing. The little girl had been riding him only a couple of weeks when, as his owner put it, he began to "show his spots." By the time I saw the little horse, the family had owned him for about a year and were dead set against owning him for another one.

"Paints," the horse's owner grunted, as we stood looking at the little gelding. "The only thing worse than a paint horse is a small paint horse. At least you can make a pack horse out of big ones."

"Not a paint fan, huh?" I questioned.

"I can't stand 'em," he replied. "Never could. If you ask me, they're nothin' but trouble wrapped up in a fancy package. We would have never even gotten this one if I'd anything to say about it."

"Really," I commented. "How'd you end up with him then?"

"I was out of town when my wife and daughter found him." He was shaking his head. "They bought him and brought him home before I even knew what had happened. I told 'em not to buy a paint, but they didn't listen. Of course, now look who they leave it to, to get rid of the dang thing."

"Isn't that always the way?" I replied in the most sympathetic voice I could muster without sounding completely patronizing. "Could you show me how he works?"

"Sure," he smiled. "But I can tell you right now, he works just like every other paint that you've probably ever seen."

The little horse definitely had some problems. However, after watching the horse being ridden and worked, I was fairly confident that all his problems were relatively superficial and certainly fixable, providing, of course, that Kristie and I were willing to spend a little time with him. So, with that in mind, we worked out a deal and got him bought.

We took the little horse up to the ranch and gave him a few days to settle in and get used to the place before we got started with him. When we finally did start working with him, it was Kristie who was in the saddle, not me. This was due in part to the fact that Kristie's smaller frame fit the horse much better than mine. But, more importantly, it was because Kristie, who had been watching and helping me work with several horses over the last couple of years and who was an excellent hand with horses in her own right, wanted very much to try to work through this horse's problems on her own.

Unfortunately for Kristie, the first few days of working with the horse were filled with nothing but frustration. Besides all the bad behavior that we already knew about, he quickly showed us a couple of other things that he wasn't real fond of doing. He exhibited two main problems—his lack of willingness to have his feet picked up and, even more important, his absolute refusal to go away from the gate once he had passed through it and was inside the arena. When Kristie finally did get him to leave the gate, he would simply take the first opportunity that came along and bolt back to it. Once he was back, he would again lock up and refuse to leave.

When Kristie asked me what to do about the paint not wanting to leave the gate, I explained to her that sometimes horses become barn sour or, in this case, gate sour, not so much because they want to be back at the barn, but rather because they don't want to be where they are. In other words, if a horse is uncomfortable in the arena, whether it's physical or mental discomfort, it only makes sense that it won't want to stay there. The problem then is not so much how to get the horse away from the gate but to figure out why it's so uncomfortable that it doesn't want to leave the gate.

Together we discussed several possibilities that might cause the paint to act the way he did. The one thing that we both agreed on was that he was quite unresponsive to anything that he was asked to do. This seemed to hint that perhaps he wasn't as well trained as everyone had thought. If that was in fact the case, then there was no need to wonder why he was acting so belligerently. The paint not only had no idea of how to do the things we were asking him to do, he didn't even know what it was we were asking.

With that in mind, Kristie began to take a little different tack with the horse. After taking him into the arena, she slowly began to show him what was expected of him instead of trying to force him to do what was expected of him (as some people might with a horse that knew what it was supposed to do but was simply refusing to do it). Even so, he didn't show much improvement for the first couple of days. While still a bit frustrated, Kristie remained consistent in what she did and how she did it, and after about a week's time, the little horse began to show signs that he was coming around. Not only was he beginning to respond to Kristie's cues and do what she was asking, his attitude began to make a complete turnaround as well. He was slowly becoming more willing to do things that before would have simply been out of the question, and his bad habits, such as bucking, rearing, and locking up any time he passed the gate, had all but disappeared.

Soon Kristie was guiding trail rides off him and using him to give riding lessons. About two months after she began working with him, she was confident enough in his abilities that she was able to put guests on him and use him for trail rides. Now, several years later, he has become so friendly and responsive that he is one of the most requested horses on the ranch, and Kristie still refers to him as "my little pony." Not a bad ending, I think, for a horse that had the misfortune of being born with two strikes against him—being small and being a paint.

I would hate to have to guess how many horses I've seen that fall into the same category as that little horse. Ones that have been given up on by someone because they weren't the right breed, color, or size. Ones that, if they aren't lucky enough to fall into sympathetic and caring hands, never get a chance to prove what they could have made of themselves simply because of the way they look. It's too bad, because many of those horses end up either getting a one-way trip to the slaughter house or seem never to meet their potential and bounce around from one disgruntled owner to the next.

A while ago I happened to have a chance to see one such horse, a horse that seemed to have so many things going against him that giving up on him may have arguably been the best option. The horse was a small, two-year-old appaloosa that was owned by a friend of mine, Dan Howes, up in Wisconsin. Dan had been working during the summers as a wrangler at the ranch where I worked and had decided to bring the horse along one summer to get his training started. Up to that point the horse had had very minimal handling. His training had consisted of being caught, haltered, and led, but just barely. His first introduction to a trailer was when he was loaded into a two-horse with the center partition removed, then hauled the 900 or so miles from Wisconsin to the ranch.

Upon his arrival he simply refused to get out of the dang thing, and getting him comfortable enough to want to get out took nearly forty-five minutes. I saw the little horse for the first time on the day after he arrived and couldn't believe how similar his actions and mannerisms were to those of wild mustangs. He was very alert and aware of everyone and everything around him and he didn't seem to like any of it. For instance, the simple act of walking up to his water tank or feed trough seemed to scare him to death and, for him, appeared to be a major accomplishment. When he approached either one, he took on the appearance of a giraffe on skates. He would hold his head low to the ground, stretching his neck out as far as it would go, then inch ever so slowly and carefully up toward the trough, while blowing hard through his nose and bobbing his head up and down. It was almost as if he was trying to warn the thing that he was coming up to it and at the same time praying with everything he had that it wouldn't attack him when he did. I just kind of assumed that this behavior was due mainly to the fact that he was in a completely unfamiliar place. I felt fairly certain that if we gave him a few days to settle in, he'd calm right down and we could get started with his training. However, I soon found that assumption to be more that just a little bit wrong. It seemed like the longer he was there and the more someone tried to work with him, the worse he got.

He was so bad, in fact, that simply trying to get him caught might take an hour or two and the act of touching or petting him would often send him into a complete panic. To make matters worse, the little horse had yet to be gelded, and with all the mares on the ranch coming into their heat cycles, he was all of a sudden trying to act like a stallion.

There was no question in my mind that he had absolutely no trust, confidence, or respect for anything that walked on two legs, and it didn't seem as though he had any wish to try developing any of those qualities. Unfortunately, the act of gelding him, which was inevitable, was probably not going to do a thing to help bolster his motivation for doing so, either. After all, looking at it from his point of view, I doubt that I'd get a warm, fuzzy feeling for anybody or anything that would intentionally hurt me, especially if I didn't care much for them to begin with.

At any rate, two weeks after he arrived at the ranch, Dan's horse found himself being led from the pen that had become his home into the large, grassy arena near the barn. Waiting for him there was the local vet armed with all the instruments he would need to perform the necessary surgery. As Dan brought the young horse down the narrow road that led from his pen to the barn area, I noticed the horse walking in a most peculiar way. It was the type of movement that I had once heard the old man refer to as "ringy." This term usually meant that the horse moved like he wasn't all there—that something was wrong with him, mentally. As he moved, all four of his legs were spread very wide apart and each step he took appeared cautious and calculated, as if he were walking through a mine field. His head snaked from side to side as he walked, as though he was making sure that if anything was going to attack him, he'd see it and be ready to jump. Just to make sure he was ready if something did attack him, he kept every muscle in his body as tense as he could and practiced his "getaway jump" several times between his pen and his destination.

Upon entering the arena, he began acting as if his life were on the line, shying and jumping at every little thing. His reaction to the vet trying to sedate him was as bad as could be expected, with him snorting and jumping every time the needle got close to him. It took several unsuccessful attempts and a tremendous amount of coaxing, but the colt did finally stand still long enough to be injected and it wasn't long afterwards that the sedation took effect and we were able to lay him down. Once he was down, the operation went virtually without a hitch. Before finishing up, the vet took every precaution, as he always did with that type of operation, to limit the amount of bleeding the horse would experience after the surgery. When the surgery was over and the horse was up and moving around, everything appeared quite normal. Dan kept the little horse in the arena for about an hour following the surgery just to make sure he was all right, and other than appearing a little sleepy, he seemed to be back to his old self. Once he was back in his pen, he went right up to his feeder and began eating as if nothing had ever happened.

Later that night, however, complications set in. The colt had not only lost his appetite and quit drinking, but the drops of blood that are normally emitted from the incision following this type of surgery had suddenly turned into a steady stream. The colt was leaving puddles of blood everywhere he stood. Knowing, of course, that this wasn't normal, Dan immediately called the vet back out to have a look, and upon his arrival, the vet quickly and successfully went about the business of getting the bleeding stopped. He told Dan to get in touch with him if the colt didn't show signs of improvement by the next day.

At about 10:30 the next morning, Dan asked me to go up and have a look at the colt to see what I thought of his progress. Before I even got next to the pen I could see that he was definitely in trouble. He still hadn't been eating or drinking and, as a result, was becoming dangerously dehydrated. This was confirmed by the fact that his urine had turned a deep reddish-brown color—a sign that, because of lack of fluid in his body, the urine was becoming more concentrated. He also seemed very weak and depressed, with his head hanging so low that his nose almost touched the ground, and he had a general lack of interest in anything that was going on around him.

Once again, the vet was called out. This time the little horse's prognosis was less than uplifting. It appeared that he'd lost considerably more blood than was originally thought the night before and, because of that, he was in dire need of fluid replacement. If that wasn't done within the next several hours, the horse probably wouldn't last through the night. The biggest problem was that neither the local vet nor the ranch had the facilities to tend to the horse's needs properly. He not only needed an immediate influx of IV fluids, but would also need around-the-clock care. The only place nearby that offered such services was the veterinarian teaching hospital at Colorado State University in Fort Collins, nearly sixty miles away. Unfortunately, taking a horse to the university for any reason is usually rather expensive and taking one in for an emergency, which this was, is always expensive.

Therein was the dilemma that Dan was suddenly forced to contend with. How much money should he invest in a horse that had shown virtually no sign of wanting to be anything but the uncooperative, spooky little colt that he'd always been? Once Dan did put the money into him, what kind of horse would he turn out to be, especially if his attitude didn't change? What if, in fact, this entire episode made the colt's attitude toward people even worse than it already was? Then Dan would end up with a bunch of money tied up in a horse that he couldn't do anything with—one that would be not only dangerous to himself, but also to anything and anyone that he came in contact with.

It was a very difficult decision, and one that Dan didn't feel comfortable making by himself. For that reason, and also because the horse was actually a family-owned animal, he called his father long-distance to ask his opinion. Over the next three hours, several conversations took place between Dan, his father, our local vet, and their vet in Wisconsin. The general feeling that Dan was getting was not to put any more money into the horse and either to make him as comfortable as possible or simply put him down. Dan, however, was not convinced that would be the proper thing to do and so, in the end, made the decision to spend the extra money and take the colt to Fort Collins.

Once the decision was made, Dan and the ranch owner loaded the colt in the ranch's large stock trailer and took him down to the hospital. He spent the better part of a week there, receiving all of the necessary fluids and treatment he needed to make a full recovery. By the time we picked him up and brought him back up to the ranch, he was well on his way to being back to his old self.

At first, other than having lost a little weight, there appeared to be no real change in either his physical appearance or his general attitude. He was still a little snaky and hard to get along with. However, that attitude didn't seem to last long. As soon as he could, Dan began to take the little horse out of his pen and walk him for short periods of time. He did this both to exercise the colt and to keep the swelling down that normally follows the surgery he'd been through. Within about two weeks' time, Dan and the colt had covered almost every one of the ranch's 112 acres together.

Dan began to work on things that, before, would have scared the horse to death. Little things such as touching and petting him, handling his feet, and brushing him. He also began to work with the things that the horse had simply never seen before and that, in order for him to allow himself to be ridden someday, he would have to get used to. Things like saddle blankets, saddles, bridles, and ropes. These were things that Dan didn't try to force the horse to understand by throwing them up on his back. Instead Dan simply hung them on the fence of the colt's pen and let him get used to them in his own time. By doing this, the horse was able to watch as the blankets moved when the wind blew, smell the leather of the saddle, and get used to the sight and sound the saddle made when he unknowingly pulled it off the fence as he played with the stirrups. Before long, Dan was able to take the things that were hanging on the fence and put them on the horse's back without even the slightest protest on the horse's part.

About a month after he had gotten back from the hospital, the colt was ready to start his training toward becoming a real, honest-to-goodness saddle horse. Because Dan had spent a part of every single day with the horse since its return, the horse had developed a tremendous amount of trust and respect for him, and as a result, his training seemed to go extraordinarily fast. Before long, Dan and the little appaloosa had graduated from working in the confines of the round pen to the larger space of the arena. There they would work on stops and turns, mounting and dismounting from either side, and transitions from the walk to the trot. Later the horse progressed into loping and picking up the proper leads, side-passing, and letting Dan swing a rope off him. By the end of July, Dan was leading trail rides off the horse. They were crossing water, bridges, and any other obstacle that they happened to come across.

Frankly, I had never in my life seen a horse make such a complete and total turnaround in such a short period of time. The only thing that was even remotely familiar about the horse was his looks. Other than that, the changes from when he first arrived were like night and day. He had gone from being one of the spookiest horses I'd seen in a long time to one of the quietest horses on the ranch and all in just a matter of weeks. I would not have believed it had I not seen it with my own eyes.

Dan and I had the opportunity to sit down and talk about the little horse's progress on several occasions. It was during one of those sessions that he asked if perhaps I thought the reason for the colt's sudden change of attitude was that he'd been gelded. After giving the question a little thought, I told him that I was sure that was part of it, but it seemed to me as though there was more to it. It seemed almost as if the colt knew how close he had come to dying, and that somehow he understood that the reason he was alive was that Dan had gone the extra mile for him. His turnaround in behavior could have been just his way of saying thank you. After all, what better way to gain someone's trust than to save his life?

"Do you really think that horses are smart enough to reason something like that out?" Dan asked, with kind of a perplexed look on his face.

"I don't know," I told him. "What I do know is that a horse's total make-up is geared toward its own survival. I can't believe that an animal with such strong survival instincts wouldn't know or understand when his life is slipping away. How could he not know that?"

"Okay," Dan nodded his head. "But how would he be able to associate me with him getting better?"

"I'm not sure," I told him. "But it would seem to me that if he knows when he's sick, he's also got to know when he's feeling better. If he gets to feeling just a little better each day and on each one of those days he also sees you, he could very easily think that you're the thing that is making him feel that way."

To be honest, I wasn't sure if that was the real reason for the colt's drastic change of attitude or not. What I did know, however, was that the horse's future, before he got sick, didn't look very rosy. In the two weeks that I was able to observe him prior to his surgery, he appeared to be a complete basket case. Any handling seemed to scare him to death and he appeared to have no desire whatsoever to make an effort to learn what Dan was trying to teach him. In the two weeks after the surgery, things that had terrified him before appeared to be of little or no consequence to him at all, particularly when they were presented to him by Dan. This is the one aspect of the entire situation that really got my attention. It's certainly not uncommon for a horse to become somewhat more subdued once he's gelded. However, as a rule, if he had a bad attitude toward people before the surgery, he will continue to have the same attitude after, at least for a while. That wasn't the case with this horse. After the surgery he was simply a changed animal. In my opinion, that seemed to show that perhaps there was more going on than met the eye.

Dan continued to work with the colt throughout the summer and each day the horse got just a little better. Not only was he responding very well while being ridden, but he was also doing well with all the related ground work. He was easy to catch, lead, saddle, and shoe, and when it came time to teach him how to load into a two-horse trailer for his trip back to Wisconsin, he accepted it as if he had been doing it all his life.

Three months after he first arrived at the ranch, the colt, by now called Cherokee, was loaded back in the trailer that brought him and was heading back home. Somewhere in Nebraska, as they made their way down the interstate, a big eighteen-wheeler pulled up behind them. It stayed behind them for a few miles before finally moving into the passing lane and blowing by. As the truck flew past, Dan's CB radio cracked to life.

"Hey, Pony Boy," the graveled voice barked. "I think somebody stole your good horse and replaced it with a spotted jackass."

"That is my good horse," Dan replied. "And I'm glad you got to see him. He's definitely the best one you'll ever lay your eyes on."

"Yeah, right, Pony Boy," the driver chuckled. "If a stupid appy is your best horse, I'd sure hate to see your worst one."

After everything that Dan and Cherokee have been through together and all the problems they've overcome, they'll still probably face prejudice because Cherokee is an appaloosa. Unfortunately, appaloosas are perhaps the one breed in the horse world that is as equally misunderstood as the Arabian and, as a result, is equally discriminated against. Like the Arab, the appaloosa is often thought of as spooky, unmanageable, and hard to train. And as with the Arab, these accusations are often made by people who either don't understand the breed or have acquired a horse of that breed only after it has developed a number of problems. What they don't understand, perhaps, is that when it comes to working with horses, especially if you're going to work with different breeds and types, it's important to work with each one as an individual.

If you have a sensitive horse, use some sensitivity. If you have a smart horse, use some intelligence. And if you have a frightened horse, try to be soothing.

It's funny how easy it is to become prejudiced against certain breeds or types of horses. I think the reason so many people become that way is simply because everyone they know is that way. The folks that they associate with are negative about a certain breed of horse, and so they are too. When it gets right down to it, the only reason they have developed that prejudice is because of something somebody else might have said.

It's kind of like the old fable, "The King's New Clothes." It's the story of a king who buys a beautiful new suit of invisible clothes that only very smart people can see. Of course there are no clothes, but because the king doesn't want to appear stupid, he puts on the invisible clothes and parades up and down the main street. By the time he does his little stroll, the word has been passed that only smart people can see the clothes and so all the townspeople act as though they, too, can see them. Finally, the king walks past a small boy who hasn't heard about the clothes. The boy takes one look at the king and wonders out loud why he is walking up and down the street in his birthday suit.

According to the story, it took one small boy with a little common sense who hadn't been corrupted by the lie about the clothes to open everybody's eyes to something that, deep down, they already knew. There were no clothes.

I think it's very much the same when it comes to horses. Many people who say they don't like this breed or that breed or would never buy this size horse or that color of horse have never owned one to begin with. They have little or no basis for what they're saying. They are repeating what someone has told them. I think that all it might take to change a person's mind would be for someone to say what he or she already knows deep down. That is the simple fact that a good horse is a good horse, no matter what breed, color, size, or sex it happens to be. It is the people who continue to keep their minds closed to that fact who will never know just how many good horses they may have overlooked in the past, or how many more they will overlook in the future.

PART TWO

The Business End

Horse Breakers,
Trainers, and Teachers

I HAD JUST finished up with my morning chores when I heard the wheezing, popping, and banging of the old Ford as it tried to come to life. Knowing that the only reason the old man ever started the truck was so he could go to town, I went around to the front of the barn to see if he had any instructions for me before he left. He had just finished lighting a cigarette as he sat behind the wheel and was returning his heavy Zippo lighter to its usual spot in the watch pocket of his jeans, when he noticed me coming around the corner. As the truck bounced up and down, the way it always did right after it was started, and belched blue smoke from the tailpipe, which was broken somewhere under the box, he slowly made two sweeping gestures with his hand, signaling me to get in.

It had rained hard the night before, and because the window on the passenger side of the old truck never did close properly, the seat on that side was always saturated following such a storm. It was strange, too, that it was usually on those days, when the seat was soaked, that the old man would suddenly decide that it was time for me to accompany him as he went to the hardware store, tack shop, or implement dealer. On that particular day, however, his destination was completely unknown—at least to me.

After wrestling with the passenger-side door for the usual minute and a half that it took to get it open, I was finally able to get in and settle down into the seat that could have doubled as a well-used sponge. Once I was set, the old man ground the transmission until it uncooperatively surrendered and slipped into one of the gears that still worked from time to time. He maneuvered the old truck around in the yard until we were able to get back on the driveway and slowly bump and splash our way down to the gate where he stopped to let me out. By slamming my shoulder into the door three or four times in just the right spot, I could usually get it opened in a relatively short period of time. I left it open just a crack while I opened the gate and the old man drove through. By doing that, I wouldn't have to waste another minute and a half wrestling with it when I got back in again.

Once we were through the gate and out on the main road, he pulled a small, crumpled piece of paper out of his shirt pocket and handed it to me.

"Go ahead and read the address off for me," he said, over the rattle and clanging of the truck.

I opened up the paper and read off two names that had been penciled in, apparently in haste. On the other side of the paper was the address of a place out on some back road that I'd never heard of. As I read off the address, the old man nodded his head, as if he suddenly remembered where it was we were going.

"These guys have a couple of horses for sale," he said, as he nodded. "I thought we'd go over and see if they have anything we can't live without."

I nodded my head in approval, as if the final say as to where we were going was actually up to me.

"I was told they have some pretty well-bred horses that they're selling pretty cheap," he continued, as he took the last drag from his cigarette and mashed the butt out on the steering wheel. "I'm kind of interested to find out why."

We drove for quite a while, it seemed, down a bunch of gravel roads that I'd never been on before. Finally, we came upon a dirt driveway that had been turned into a pothole-filled mud bath by the storm the night before. The driveway was about three-hundred yards long and led up to an old farm house. By driving a little faster than he normally would, dodging the potholes, and staying out of the shallow drainage ditches that ran on either side of the driveway, we were able to get up to the farm house in relatively short order. Somebody else, it appeared, hadn't been so lucky. Tire tracks led off the driveway and out about forty feet into the field, where an old Chevy pickup was buried in the mud clear up to its running boards. The front bumper had been torn off and was laying about twenty feet in front of the truck. Attached to the bumper was a heavy log chain that led to an elderly International Harvester tractor. It, too, was hopelessly stuck in the muddy field, buried almost to its back axle.

We had no sooner pulled up to the house than two mud-caked, long-haired dogs ran up, barking and wagging their tails. The dogs were followed by a large-bellied man in his fifties, wearing dirty jeans, rumpled shirt, and about a week's worth of beard. His ball cap was tipped off to the side and he was wiping his hands with a rag that was so dirty that I couldn't believe it was doing any good.

"Mornin'," he said, with a smile that showed off his three remaining front teeth. "What can I do for ya?"

"We heard you've got some horses for sale," the old man said with a smile. "We thought we'd come on out and see if you had anything we could use."

"You bet," the fellow nodded. "We got a bunch of real good colts. Come on down and I'll show you what we got."

As I climbed out of the truck, I noticed that the dampness of the truck seat had been absorbed by the seat of my pants. Normally, this

would have embarrassed me due to the resemblance it presented of someone who had wet his pants. However, as we made our way behind the large barn toward the back of the yard, I came to realize that the folks around there, even if they did notice the large wet spot on my backside, wouldn't have cared if, in fact, I actually had wet my pants.

"That danged ol' number one son of mine, Warren, got himself all liquored up last night," the fellow said, as the old man and I dodged and sidestepped the puddles that he seemed completely oblivious to. "He got home in the middle of that storm and drove his truck smack out into the field. Tried to use the old binder to pull it out. Worked on it for over an hour, I guess, before he finally realized that he'd pulled the bumper off and the tractor was stuck."

"Well," the old man said, as he glanced at me and shrugged his shoulders, "that does happen sometimes, I guess."

"Doesn't it, though?" the fellow replied, as if it were a common occurrence.

We made our way out behind the barn to several small, square corrals, all with horses in them. A young fellow on a large bay gelding was in one of the corrals, and with him were two boys in their late teens or early twenties, one holding a spade shovel, the other holding a broom.

"This dang old jughead," the man grunted, as we walked up to the pen. "He just don't want to get broke. He keeps rearing up."

The horse suddenly did just that. The rider pulled hard on his mouth while kicking him with his spurs, and the horse stood straight up on his back legs. The rider quickly jumped off, landing on his feet, and pulled hard on the left rein, which tipped the horse off balance, sending him crashing over backwards and throwing him on his right side in the mud. The rider continued to pull on the left rein, which kept the horse's head tipped nearly back to the saddle horn. This forced him to lie on his side, unable to get up. While he lay helplessly on the ground, the other two fellows in the pen quickly ran up and began beating him mercilessly with the shovel and broom, while the man who was holding the rein in one hand began beating him with the riding crop he was holding in the other. All three were yelling and screaming at the tops of their lungs while the horse struggled unsuccessfully to get up. After what seemed like an eternity, they finally quit the impromptu flogging and allowed the horse to scramble to his feet. They let him stand for only a short time before the man got back on.

He threw himself quickly into the saddle and spurred the horse forward. The horse had gone only a short distance when the rider jerked him to a stop. Again, the horse reared, and again he was pulled over backwards and beaten. This whole process was repeated at least three more times while we were standing there before the horse finally gave up and quit rearing.

"Warren," the father called to the fellow riding the horse as soon as it stopped without rearing. "These boys have come to look at some horses. Show 'em what we got."

The father turned, shook the old man's hand, and nodded. "Warren'll show ya around. I don't do much ridin' no more since I got pregnant." He laughed out loud while slapping his distended belly. "Let me know if you see anything you like."

"I sure will," the old man nodded with a smile. "Thanks."

Over the next two hours Warren showed us six different horses. In order to get any of them caught, we either had to corner them, bribe them with grain, or in a couple of cases, rope them. Once a horse was caught, Warren brought it out of its pen, tied it to a large hitch rail, and threw a saddle and bridle on it. I couldn't help but notice, as all this was going on, that all the horses appeared to have one thing in common— they all appeared to be terrified of people. If you walked up alongside one of them, it would shy away from you. If you walked up behind the horse, it would jump forward, and if you walked anywhere near one's head as it stood tied, it would automatically and uncontrollably pull back. Any time one of the horses had one of these reactions, either Warren or one of the other fellows who had come over to give him a hand would reprimand the animal by immediately yelling and then hitting it.

All the horses were well behaved while being ridden, although they were very stiff and rigid in everything they did. They held their heads relatively high, while they kept their eyes wide open and continually chomped at the bit. Each of the horses could go from a stop to a fast lope at the snap of a finger and then from the lope to a sliding stop just as quickly. They could also spin a fast circle in either direction, would stand to be mounted from either side, and allowed themselves to be roped off of. I also noticed that, while they all did what they were told, when they were told to do it, they didn't do it every time they were told to. In other words, about every third or fourth time that the rider would ask one of them to stop, turn, or back, the horse would simply refuse. This refusal usually resulted in some form of punishment from the rider. The horse would either be spurred, have its bit jerked on, or be slapped on the neck or butt with the reins. Sometimes the punishment would be a combination of all three, without the slightest sign of leniency from the rider. It was soon quite obvious that any kind of refusal on the part of the horse would be met with swift and uncompromising retribution.

This was apparently not only the rule of thumb for their older horses, but also for the less well trained, younger ones as well. The last horse that Warren brought out was a three-year-old filly that he had only started working with two days earlier. The little horse appeared even more terrified than the others had as he threw his heavy roping saddle up on her back. She shied and tried to scoot out from underneath it as soon as he started to swing it over her back. When that happened, he yelled loudly and kicked her squarely in the belly. She fought desperately to get away but, in the end, finally stood, shaking with fear, and allowed him to throw the saddle on her back.

"She's still pretty dumb," he said, after getting up in the saddle. "But we got a good start on her. I think she'll be easy to finish up if you're looking for something to play around with for a few months."

Warren kicked the little mare five or six times lightly with his spurs to urge her forward. Her only response each time was a jerking of her entire body. Because she didn't respond the way he wanted her to, he kicked her hard with the spurs. She responded by jumping almost straight up in the air, then bucking once she came back to the ground. She bucked up one side of the corral, then down the other, before he was finally able to get her pulled up. He then slapped her several times with the reins while spurring her and pulling her around in a circle. For the next half-hour, Warren herded the little mare around the corral, jerking her head around when she didn't respond to neck reining, kicking her hard when she didn't go forward at just the right time, and pulling back with all his might and sawing back and forth on the reins when she didn't stop right away. The little horse, after that half-hour, was not only ringing wet from sweat, but also appeared so tired that she could hardly hold her head up.

"What have you got to have for her?" the old man asked, when Warren finally climbed down.

"You'll have to ask Pa," he replied, loosening the cinch and pulling his saddle off her. "But I think he'll probably want to get two or three hundred out of her."

The old man nodded, thanked Warren for his time, then went looking for the father. In less than fifteen minutes, the two had worked out a deal on the little mare, which included her delivery to the old man's place, and we were back in the truck and headed for home.

"They were sure hard on those horses," I said, even before we had reached the end of the driveway.

"Some people are that way," he replied, pulling out onto the road. "That's why the horses acted the way they did, all jumpy and scared. That's why they'd lock up every once in a while, too."

"Lock up?" I questioned.

"They'd all of a sudden quit doing whatever it was they were doing." He pulled out a cigarette and lit it. "They'd turn three times in a row real good, then on the fourth time, they wouldn't turn at all. They'd back up real good one time, then the next time they wouldn't even try. One time they'd move as soon as the fellow would touch 'em with his heels, the next time he'd have to kick 'em three or four times to get 'em to move at all."

"Being hard on 'em causes that?" I asked.

The old man thought for a while, then said, "It's just like when you're in school. If your teacher asked a question that you didn't know the answer to, would you want her to help you figure out the right answer or would you rather have her hit you with a stick until you guessed the right one?"

"I'd want her to help me," I replied. "I sure wouldn't want her to hit me."

"So," he said, after taking a long drag from the cigarette, "do you think a horse might learn better by somebody showing him how to do things, or by beating him until he guesses what the person wants?"

"By the person showing him," I told him.

"I agree," he said, nodding his head. "But if you don't do that, chances are the horse is going to lock up from time to time. That's what happened to those horses back there. Nobody ever showed them what they were supposed to be doing, but they were beat anyway whenever they didn't do it. The horses were forced to guess what it was the rider was looking for, and as a result, they never really knew when they were doing the right thing. They didn't know if a kick in the sides meant to go forward, backward, or if they were just being punished again. They didn't know if pressure on the reins meant to turn, stop, back up, or stand still." He shook his head slowly from side to side. "It's got to be a real confusing way for a horse to try to learn."

"Scary too," I added.

He went on to explain that horses that have been trained in such a way usually end up being pretty high-strung for most of their lives, even after they go to a different home. He said that, because the horse is always "waiting for the other shoe to drop," no matter who is riding it, it's constantly on edge. This, of course, keeps the rider on edge, which only serves to compound the problem.

"There are an awful lot of horses out there that have been trained that way," he said. "They're usually easy to pick out in a crowd, too. They're the ones wearing the tie-downs, chomping at the bit, and that never want to stand still."

"If that's the case," I asked, "then how come you bought that filly?"

"Well," he smiled, "we need a few more horses. We probably could have bought some of those others and quieted them down enough to work with 'em, but it would have taken awhile. On the other hand, they'd only worked the filly a few times, so the damage to her shouldn't be quite as bad. She should come around a whole lot faster and be something we could use in a couple of months." He paused for a second, still smiling. "Besides, I really liked the looks of her."

Warren and his father delivered the little filly about mid-morning the next day. As she came out of the trailer, I couldn't help thinking that perhaps the old man had made a mistake when he bought her. She was hard to handle and very jumpy. She even tried to run off on three different occasions before they got her to her pen. Once she was inside the pen, she ran up and down one side with her head over the top rail, screaming as loud as she could. She continued to pace and scream for the rest of that day and half of the next before finally quieting down some.

I remember mentioning to the old man that she didn't seem to be settling down much and that maybe we would have been better off with one of those older horses. They may have been a little jumpy and somewhat unresponsive to ride, but they probably wouldn't have taken the move as hard as this young filly had. The old man listened intently as I expressed my doubts about the horse, and when I was finished, he tipped his hat back and scratched his head.

"I'll tell you what," he said, appearing as though he'd been deep in thought over what I'd said. "Let's give her a couple more days, then we'll see where she's at before we worry too much."

Of course, as it turned out, he was right. Over the next two days, the little horse settled down considerably, and within a week he was actually working with her. Within two weeks, she had done quite a turnaround. She was still a long way from going out on the trail or working in the arena, mind you, but her change of attitude was astonishing.

It wasn't until a month or two later, after I'd been watching and helping the old man work with the filly, that it dawned on me just how good he really was with horses. The change in her was so complete that it seemed as though the little filly that he'd originally bought no longer existed. In that horse's place was this friendly, well-mannered, and well-trained colt that would happily do anything that you asked of her, and the only reason she was that way was because of the way she was treated and handled by the old man. Oh, I think I always had an idea that there was something special about the way he worked with horses. But until I'd gotten a chance to see this horse and how she'd been treated before we got her, I never had anything to compare it to. I guess when it came right down to it, I'd been leading a pretty sheltered life when it came to horses and how other people handled them.

At the time he acquired this little horse, I'd been working for the old man for about three years. During that time I'd seen an awful lot of horses come and go, many of them with problems a lot worse than the filly. The big difference was that I'd never actually seen the horse's problems being caused before; the horses always had the problems before they got to us. Because of that, I guess I just assumed that they had always been that way and that their behavior was really nobody's fault. Because the old man's way of working horses was the only method I'd been exposed to, I figured that most people who worked with horses handled them and had the same compassion for them as he did. Surely nobody would go out of their way to try to get their horses to act badly. What sense would that make? Why would anybody want to handle a horse in such a way as to cause and promote unwanted behavior, especially to the point where they'd end up having to get rid of the horse because of it? I just couldn't believe that anyone would purposely do something like that. I still can't.

I must admit, however, that getting a chance to watch Warren and the boys work their horses was a tremendous eye-opening experience for me. It showed me a whole side to horse training that I had never been exposed to before. It showed me the "do it or else" attitude of the horse *breaker*—a person with the idea that horses are tools and nothing more, and that overpowering the animal instead of trying to work with it is how you make it into what you want. It also helped me to understand how and why bad behavior is developed and promoted. Even more importantly, it gave me a whole new outlook and respect for the old man, what he did, and how he did it.

From that time on, I'd just assumed that the "do it or else" attitude that I became familiar with that day was being perpetuated solely by the horse breakers of the world—people who did a poor job in the initial training of the horse. It dawned on me only a few years ago that such is not the case.

I was leaning against the rail fence of the outdoor arena, sipping on a cold Mountain Dew and talking with a client whose horse we'd just finished working, when a little girl led her old gelding through the gate of the arena and mounted up. She was followed closely by a small, dark-haired woman in her mid-twenties who made a slow pass around the horse, apparently checking his tack. When the woman was confident that everything was properly adjusted, she looked up at the girl and with a smile, told her to take the horse to the rail and let him walk off. The little girl, who was also smiling, responded immediately to the request.

For the next five minutes or so, the woman, who, as it turned out, was the girl's riding instructor, called out some very simple commands to the girl. Each time the little girl responded by doing what she was told. The commands that the woman gave consisted of asking the pair to walk forward, stop, back a few steps, then reverse direction. When they were doing those things well, the instructor asked the girl to move her horse into a trot, which the pair did flawlessly. The little girl, who seemed to be having trouble holding back her smile, responded to all the commands as quickly as she could while trying hard to keep her body in the proper riding position—back straight, heels down, shoulders square. This was obviously something she'd been practicing, and by the look on her face, she was sure she was doing it properly.

"Very good, Annie," the woman called in a cheery voice. "Are we ready to try a lope?"

The girl, still with her eyes focused forward, and smiling like the Cheshire cat, nodded her head.

"Okay," the instructor said, as she put her hands behind her back. "Give him a little squeeze with your heels."

From where I was standing, I could see the girl's legs moving closer to the horse's sides, but there was no response from the horse.

"Try again," the woman called. Again, there was no response from the horse.

"Okay, Annie," the woman called, this time with a slight edge to her voice. "Give him a kick."

The horse responded to the kick by loping a few feet then falling back into a trot.

"Kick him again, Annie. This time, real hard."

That, I'm afraid, was the beginning of the end. For the next half-hour, because of the horse's refusal to lope, Annie's riding lesson turned into little more than a street brawl between her and the animal. Her instructor was standing in the middle of the arena, yelling at her the entire time to hit and kick the horse with everything she had.

"Don't let him get away with that," she hollered in a voice so loud that it even took me by surprise. "If you aren't going to make him do what you want, then you might as well get off of him."

The instructor soon went to the barn and brought back a riding crop, handed it to Annie, and told her if the horse still didn't mind, to whack him hard with that. The horse's only response to being hit with the crop was to trot a little faster and halfheartedly buck. That was more than the instructor could bear. She went over and got Annie off the horse. She mounted up and proceeded to kick, hit, slap, jerk, and cuss the horse until he finally broke into a lope. Once he had loped a time or two around the arena, she gave the horse back to the little girl. The only problem was that they ended up right back where they started from, with Annie hitting and kicking the horse with everything she had and the horse using just as much energy to refuse her request.

Another fifteen minutes of futile attempts passed before the instructor finally allowed Annie to quit. The look the little girl had as she left the arena was a stark change from the beaming face she had taken in with her, and I couldn't help but feel sorry for her as she walked her horse slowly past the spot where I was standing. She had the look of a child who had been totally defeated. A fate that, in my opinion, no child should be subjected to no matter what the circumstances, but especially not when dealing with a horse.

It was also obvious that she was leaving the arena with two thoughts. The first was that the horse had beat her. He had gotten the better of her, and she couldn't get him to do what she wanted. That look was all over her face. The second was something that had shown on her face when she was in the arena. It was the thought she had when she saw how her instructor acted when she got on the horse. The instructor was both physically and verbally abusive to the animal, and in the little girl's eyes, even though it looked and sounded bad, it got the job done. I can't help but wonder what kind of message that sent to the little girl. What did it say to her about what was acceptable behavior when she faced a similar problem in the future? Did it encourage her to try to find out why a horse acts the way it does and then look for a solution, or did it tell her that the solution to any problem with a horse is to use force?

I have been very fortunate in that I've had the opportunity to watch a number of great horse trainers and riding instructors over the years and, after observing each one of the really good ones, it seems to me they all have one thing in common. Even though their methods and styles may differ, they all appear to have a genuine compassion for the horse and a willingness to work with the animal instead of against it. They're the ones who always seem to find a way to get through to the horse and who are able to get a horse to do what they're asking because it wants to, not because it has to. They're the ones who use their ability to communicate with the animal more than they use their ability to force the animal and, in fact, they look at force as an absolute last resort in even the worst situations.

I recall going to a clinic some time ago where the trainer was given a horse that absolutely refused to load in a trailer. The horse was so bad that he would rear and strike whenever he got anywhere near one. I remember thinking, as the trainer brought him close to the trailer for the first time, that this was going to be a project that was going to take a while, if it got done at all, because the horse didn't seem in any way willing to take part in the day's activities and fought like crazy whenever he got within thirty feet of the trailer door.

The trainer appeared undaunted by the task and went about his business as if it were a leisurely stroll through the park. Within thirty minutes, he had the horse standing quietly at the door. Within an hour and fifteen minutes, he had the horse going in and out of the trailer completely on his own. After an hour and a half, the trainer went over and took a seat in the driver's side of the pickup that the trailer was hooked to. With the horse on a sixty-foot rope and standing next to him, he closed the truck door. He then sent the horse, on its own, to the back of the trailer. The horse made a large sweeping circle on his way to the trailer door, and yet, with the trainer still sitting in the truck, he simply walked up and loaded himself. The trainer never once raised his voice or his hand to the horse the entire time he was working with him. In my opinion, that made a pretty strong case for the argument that communication is better than force.

Unfortunately, for each one of the good trainers that I've seen over the years, I've seen just as many bad ones. There is one person in particular that stands out in my mind as the type of person who truly has no business being around horses. Not that he wasn't a fair hand, mind you, but because of the damage that he did in other ways. He was the type of person you run into from time to time in the horse business and each time you do, you hope that you never do again. He was the type of person who appears very honest, talented, and knowledgeable, and who uses those traits to befriend his unsuspecting victims.

The fellow had come to the area from somewhere out on the West Coast and apparently brought a great deal of money with him. He was a tall, friendly fellow who wore a great big Tom Mix style hat, red high-top boots into which he tucked his pants, and large rowled spurs that jingled any time he moved. As soon as he got to town he bought himself a little horse ranch and acquired several high-dollar show horses. He also began going to horse auctions and buying up other horses, mostly grade horses that he brought to his place and either let people use to trail ride or that he turned around and sold.

Every chance he got over the next couple of years, he dropped the names of several well-known show-horse trainers he had apparently been associated with. These were people he'd bought horses from in the past, and who had helped him show and win. He talked often of his many victories in the show ring and of all the nationally ranked horses he had owned in the past. He also talked of how highly respected he had become over the years, especially in certain circles involving the horse show industry, and how, because of all the great horses he'd sold in all his years in the business, he'd become known as the man to come to whenever someone wanted to buy a horse.

It wasn't long before he was advertising in the local paper that he was not only selling and dealing in "quality" horses, but that he was also providing horse boarding, training, and giving riding lessons at his place as well. This is where his two years of self-promotion paid off. Soon his barn was filled with the horses of paying customers who were boarding their horses with him, having their horses trained, or taking riding lessons.

Unfortunately, his actual knowledge of horses and his true agenda for owning them would soon become apparent. Of the three horses that he'd taken in for training, none were improving. In fact, in each case, they were getting worse. One little horse, a small black mare, had not only become very hard to handle but had bucked him off a time or two. He ended up telling the owner that he thought the horse was crazy and that she should sell her, which she did a couple of weeks later. Before she took the horse to the auction, however, the fellow talked her into drugging the horse so it would appear quiet and docile in the sale ring and would bring more money. When she protested, he simply told her that drugging was a very common practice and that everybody did it. Of course that wasn't true, but because she didn't know any better, the owner agreed.

One of the other horses that he was working, a large bay gelding, had also developed some pretty bad behavior. Shaking his head, bucking, and rearing were just a few of his newly acquired problems. The fellow told the owner that the horse needed to understand who was boss, so he had taken to jerking on the horse's head, beating, and spurring it. The horse was being trained in a bosal, a type of bit where the brunt of the pressure from the rider's hands is on the bridge of the horse's nose. Because of how roughly he had treated the horse, he had literally rubbed the horse's face raw in just a matter of minutes. This horse, because of its drastic "mood swings," as the fellow explained to the owner after a few weeks, was also deemed worthless. It was sold about a month and a half later.

The third horse, a paint gelding, quickly developed problems similar to the first two. However, that horse's owner was very attached to the animal and simply refused to sell it, even after several long, heated discussions in which the fellow described in detail the worthlessness of the animal. Two weeks following their last discussion on the subject, the horse suddenly and mysteriously died during the night.

Luckily, for each one of the owners, the fellow just happened to have a few "real good" horses for sale. These horses, he said, were all very well bred and were out of registered stock. The only problem was that, due to some wacky bureaucratic mix-up, these particular horses no longer had registration papers and so had to be sold without them. They were still worth more than just any old horse, due of course, to their alleged blood lines. So naturally he would need to charge more for them than he would, had they not been out of registered stock.

Each of the owners was relatively new to the horse business and all were well-off financially. All three took the fellow at his word because he seemed so honest and knowledgeable, and as a result, they all bought horses from him to replace the ones they lost. Out of the three horses that he sold to them, two came up lame almost immediately after they were purchased. Of course, when the owners confronted the fellow about it, he simply told them that he'd sold the horses "as is." He was sure sorry that the horses weren't sound anymore, but there wasn't a thing he could do about it. That was the horse business.

Unfortunately, the truth of the matter is, he was right. In the eyes of the law, he really hadn't done anything wrong. Oh, I guess an argument could be made that, as a trainer, he had made their horses worse. But there's no law against being a bad horse trainer. Besides, the horses that he had perhaps ruined were long gone. So, even if there were a law against being a bad trainer, there was no way for anyone to prove that he'd done any damage. As far as selling lame horses, if he didn't guarantee the horses sound before the sale, legally he wasn't responsible for making good on them after the sale. Basically, it was a simple case of let the buyer beware.

It's sad, but one of the biggest problems with the horse industry is that it lends itself to an unscrupulous person taking advantage of unsuspecting and trusting people. He or she doesn't care about people and cares even less about horses. The one thing an unscrupulous person does care about is how much money can be made off both, and he'll use his ability to gain people's trust to milk them for everything he can.

The good news is that there are ways of guarding against being taken advantage of—the best way is the simple use of a little common sense. The thing I always tell people is not to take anything a trainer tells you as gospel. If what the trainer is saying or doing doesn't sound or look right to you, ask about it. If the answer doesn't sound right, question the answer. Always be aware of what your horse is going through and ask to be a part of the training process. If the trainer doesn't want you to be around while your horse is being worked, look at that as a red flag and something that you should be concerned about.

Second, I suggest to folks that they set realistic goals with the trainer before they get started, but not to set the goals in concrete. Remember, all horses are individuals and should be treated as such. When you set your goals always leave enough room for the trainer to make adjustments, to slow down if things aren't going as well as he or she thought, or speed up if they're going better. The trainer should have a pretty good idea how far along the horse will be after one month, two months, and three months, and should be willing to make a commitment to that fact.

Third, and most important, I tell folks to look at their agreement with the trainer as a business proposition. You can be assured that's how the trainer is looking at it, so why shouldn't you? After all, if you didn't pay the training fee in a timely manner, you'd expect that your horse's training would cease. So, in my opinion, if you aren't getting the results you expected within the time frame that you agreed upon, perhaps you, as the employer, should look for another employee.

I always try to tell people who are looking for a trainer to think like a consumer. Have an idea of not only how much you want to spend, but also what you expect to get for your money. Give some thought as to what kind of trainer you're looking for, then don't give up looking until you find the right one. Think about it. Are you looking for somebody to break your horse for you, somebody who will rough him up a little if he "needs" it, or are you looking for someone to teach your horse the difference between right and wrong, someone who is willing to work from the horse's perspective?

Some years ago I had a young student who unknowingly taught me what I believe to be the most important quality that a horse trainer should possess, and it's something that I think every owner should look for. The student was a young woman whose main ambition when we started working together was to be able to train a horse from start to finish all by herself. She was a very conscientious person who asked a lot of questions, worked hard, and wasn't afraid to get her hands dirty. Together, we covered everything from how to feed a horse, to teaching a horse how to respond to leg cues, to ground driving, and virtually everything else in between and beyond. After we'd been working together for about a year, we both agreed that it was time for her to try her hand at the goal she'd been working so hard to achieve. With that, I assigned her a nice little two-year-old filly that I thought would be easy to work with. She was extremely excited to get started and rose to the occasion with the enthusiasm of a child opening presents on Christmas morning.

As I expected, she had very little trouble with the young horse and breezed right through the initial ground work. In about three weeks' time, she'd done such a good job with the filly that the little horse was ready to be ridden.

I stood at the gate of the round pen that morning as she slowly went through the filly's daily routine. After grooming, longeing, and saddling the young horse, she brought out the long driving lines and drove her from the ground. The horse responded to her effortlessly by turning, stopping, and backing with very light pressure from the lines. The young woman stopped the little horse and removed the driving lines from the bit, replacing them with a leather roping rein. She went over and checked the cinch before putting her foot in the stirrup and bouncing up and down several times. She appeared to be ready to start working her way up into the saddle when she suddenly stopped everything she was doing and stood quietly by the horse's side.

"Looks like she's ready," I said, after she'd been standing for a couple of minutes.

"I've been thinking," she said, petting the horse on the shoulder with her left hand, while propping her right hand on the saddle horn. "This is a real important time in this horse's life, isn't it?"

"What do you mean?" I asked.

"What I do here today is going to stick with her forever." There was a hint of concern in her voice.

"Yes," I responded. "I believe it will."

"I never thought about it before," she was still stroking the horse's shoulder, "but this is kind of a big responsibility."

"What is?" I asked.

"Working with these horses," she replied. "Its kind of like raising a child, isn't it? All of the good things and bad things she learns from now on, she'll be learning from me. If she ends up being a bad horse, it'll be my fault."

"I guess so," I told her. "If she ends up being a good horse, that'll be your fault, too."

She stood for a while longer as if giving the whole situation a little more thought. Then she glanced over at me, and with a smile, turned back toward the horse and climbed on.

Just like that, she had summed up what, in my opinion, it is to be a horse trainer. It's a responsibility, but not just a responsibility to the client. Even more important, it's a responsibility to the horse. After all, its future is in the trainer's hands. If the trainer produces a good horse, chances are the horse will have a good life. If the trainer produces a bad horse, chances are it'll have a bad life, if it has a life at all.

Lord knows there are a lot of horse trainers out there, some good, some not so good. I think the thing that separates the good ones from the bad ones is that the good ones understand their responsibility to both horse and owner, and I think the thing that separates a good owner from a bad one is that the good owner understands his or her responsibility to the horse. Without that understanding, it seems, the horse often becomes nothing more than another tool in the shed, a tool that is easily discarded because it never worked properly, when all it may have taken for it to be useful to begin with was for the owner to read the directions.

5

Buying a Good One

It was a Saturday morning, and even before breakfast I was in a bit of a turmoil over what I should do for the day. I had two choices. The first was to do the same thing that I did every Saturday during the fall of the year—play touch football with my friends in the nearby school yard. The second was something that I'd never done before—attend a horse auction with the old man at the local fairgrounds. It was a difficult decision as I hated to miss our weekly dose of adolescent male bonding and the chance to get my clothes dirty. But in the end, I couldn't resist the beckoning of something as exotic as horses being sold by a person who talked faster than any human has a right to.

Having made my decision, I climbed on my bike and headed for the old man's place, where he was patiently waiting for me to arrive. I helped him finish his morning chores before we hopped in the old Ford and drove the ten miles or so to the fairgrounds. The sale had not yet started when we arrived, so we quickly made our way over to the holding pens to have a look at the horses that were going to be auctioned off.

"We need three good horses," the old man said, pulling a pack of Lucky Strike cigarettes from his shirt pocket. Evidently, the store had been out of the Camels he usually smoked, and Lucky must have been the only brand he could find with the same potency. "Why don't you look around and see if you can find us three good ones?"

"Me?" I questioned.

"Sure," he answered. "There's plenty to pick from. When you find three that you can't live without, come find me. I'll be over there." He pointed to an area where there were a couple of rows of horse-drawn machinery and some harness.

"What should I look for?" I asked.

"It doesn't really matter," he shrugged. "Just anything that looks good to you."

With that, he turned and walked off toward the machinery. At first, I couldn't believe that he had left the serious task of picking the horses we were going to buy that day up to me. But after giving the matter a little thought, I decided that maybe it wasn't that strange. After all, I'd been with him quite often when he bought horses in the past, and I'd watched how he did it and what he looked for. I had a pretty good idea of the kind of horses he preferred, and having worked with him for the past three years, I felt I had developed an eye for good horseflesh, even if I did say so myself. That was probably the reason he had asked me to pick the horses. He'd probably seen how proficient a horseman I was becoming and had decided that it was time for me to take a more active role in the inner workings of the operation. Yes, that must have been it. He was starting to consider me as his equal, and picking the horses that day was simply the first step to becoming a full-fledged partner. In time, he would probably just turn the whole business over to me.

First things first, however. Before I could become a ranch owner, I first had to get these three good horses picked out—a task, I figured, that shouldn't be too difficult for someone with my vast knowledge and experience. Taking my time, I made my way over to the first pen, which held a bay quarter horse mare. I looked her over carefully, noticing that she was slightly ewe-necked and a little underweight. Probably not a horse that my partner and I would be interested in, I decided. I moved on to the next pen. It held a large, short-backed gray gelding. Standing next to me was a man in his mid-twenties who seemed very interested in the horse. After giving the gelding a quick once over with my experienced eye, I figured that being short-backed would definitely be a hindrance, and I walked away shaking my head, hoping the young man wouldn't be fool enough to put a bid in on the gelding come sale time.

I looked at several more horses, dismissing them all for various reasons, before finally coming to one that I figured would be worthy of purchasing. He was a big paint gelding, very colorful and flashy. He was standing tied with his head toward the back of the pen, obviously to show off his powerful hind quarters to prospective buyers, and he appeared to have been recently groomed, including a freshly cut bridle path. He had very good lines, whatever that meant, and his legs all appeared to be pretty straight. Yes, this would be one of the three that we would buy. I made note of the number that had been pasted on his hip and continued on my way.

Within about five minutes, I came upon the next horse that was sure to come home with us that day. He was a black gelding, a little bigger than the paint, but just as stout. He had a very quiet eye and appeared to be an easy keeper, as he seemed to be a bit overweight. He had a sweat mark on his back where a saddle had been, so I was sure he'd been ridden recently, and he had a very wide chest, similar to that of a professional roping horse. Looking around, I noticed a lot of people looking at the other horses, but none standing around him. I figured he was being overlooked because he was in a pen that was kind of out of the way, off in a remote corner. With any luck, I figured, they would

keep overlooking him and we would be the only ones bidding on him, which would probably mean we could get him fairly cheap. I made a note of the number on his hip and continued on.

I didn't have to go very far before finding number three. She was a very pretty liver-chestnut mare standing right at the fence and greeting everyone that happened to pass her way. She wasn't very big, standing maybe fourteen-and-a-half hands, but she more than made up for her size with her personality. She was very friendly and outgoing and appeared to love people. Surely, she would make a great riding horse and a wonderful addition to our herd. I noted her number and headed off to find the old man. As I made my way over toward the machinery, I noticed him heading my way.

"Found some already?" he asked, with just a hint of surprise in his voice as he met me.

"Yeah," I replied with a smile. "I think I've found a couple of real nice ones."

"Good," he nodded. "Let's go have a look."

With that, we made our way over to my first choice, the paint gelding. He was still standing with his head tied toward the back of the pen, and as we stood looking at him, I turned toward the old man to see his reaction. I was expecting to see his eyes bulging out of his head in disbelief at how well I was able to pick a good horse, but instead he had virtually no reaction at all.

"Well," I said enthusiastically, after letting him look the horse over for a few minutes, "what do you think?"

"He's colorful," he replied, taking out another cigarette and lighting it. "Is that why you picked him?"

"That was one of the reasons," I said, surprised that he would think I would be so ignorant as to pick out a horse based strictly on its color. "But the real reason was that he looks like a good riding horse. He's got this nice hip, and a bridle path, and his legs are good and straight."

"He sure does," he said, taking a drag from the cigarette. "But what else do you see here?"

"What do you mean?" I asked, as if I had already told him everything there was to know about the horse.

He stood quiet for a couple of seconds, then said, "You've seen the good things about the horse, but are there any bad things about him that you can see?"

I stared at the horse for what seemed like a long time, and for the life of me, I couldn't see a thing wrong with him.

"No," I said in response to his question. "Not really."

"Okay," he nodded. "Well, let's take a real good look at him. First, why is he tied with his head away from us?"

"To show off his hind quarters," I responded.

"Maybe," he said. "But sometimes when you see a horse tied this way, it's because of another reason. For instance, it could be that he bites, and the seller doesn't want us to know that. It could also be that the seller is trying to hide something on his face, like a little deformity, or in this horse's case, some bruising on his nose." The old man motioned for me to come over to where he was standing and pointed to the end of the horse's nose. From there, we could see pretty clearly some deep red marks.

"Those marks were probably left by a twitch," he said, "which tells us that, for whatever reason, someone thought he was acting bad enough that the only way to control him was to twitch him." He stopped for a second, taking another drag from his cigarette. "If you look real close at his bridle path, you can see that it isn't a real smooth cut. It's real uneven and choppy, which tells us that either the person that did it wasn't very good with electric clippers or they used a scissors on him. If they used a scissors, that could mean that he may be afraid of clippers and fights a lot when you try to use them on him, which could also be why they had to twitch him."

He moved over slightly, to get what seemed like a better side view of the animal. "Let's look at his feet," he said, bringing me over to his side. "His front feet look pretty good. They're in good shape and they look like they've been trimmed recently. But, if we look at his back feet," he paused, "there's quite a difference, isn't there?"

There was. While the front feet looked like they'd been cared for on a regular basis, the back ones looked like they'd never been cared for at all. They were long and splayed out with large open cracks running clear up the hoof wall and into the coronet band.

"What should that tell us?" he asked.

"That he doesn't like his back feet trimmed," I replied meekly.

"That's right," he nodded. "He's probably a kicker." He paused for a minute, evidently allowing me time for this new information to sink in. "What do you think, should we still go after him?"

"Probably not," I replied, slowly shaking my head.

"Okay," the old man mashed his cigarette on the metal gate. "Well, then, let's go have a look at them others."

We made our way over to the back corner where the black gelding stood. As we walked, I couldn't help but feel a bit foolish for overlooking the paint's obvious deficiencies. However, I was also confident as we approached the next pen that the old man wouldn't be able to find anything wrong with the black. After all, he had sweat marks on him, so at least we knew he had been ridden recently. He also wasn't tied with his head away from us, so the seller wasn't trying to hide his face, and he had shoes on all four feet. I distinctly remembered seeing that. When we got to the pen, the old man took a long hard look at the horse before saying anything.

"He's a nice-looking horse," he said matter-of-factly. "He's only got one problem, though. Can you see what it is?"

Problem. What problem? This horse didn't have any problems. This was the best horse in the place and was probably going to be the buy of the day. What did he mean he had a problem? I couldn't see any problem.

"No," I said, without really giving the horse much of a look.

"His left rear leg," he said quietly, pointing to the leg. "See it?"

I looked at the leg and, at first, didn't see anything out of the ordinary. That is, until I compared it to the other rear leg. After comparing the two, it was easy to see that there was noticeable swelling in the horse's left hock.

"I don't think he had that before," I told him.

"Oh," the old man smiled, "he probably did. Maybe you just didn't see it. It's what's called a bog spavin, a joint problem. He's actually probably had it for quite awhile."

We stood looking at the horse for a little while longer before, dejected, I turned and headed over to the mare's pen, which was only a short distance away. The old man followed quietly behind. As we reached the pen, the mare walked right up and pressed her nose to the bars in a friendly greeting.

"Well," the old man smiled, "aren't you the friendly one?"

While petting the mare on the bridge of the nose, he glanced through the bars at her body and immediately noticed something that I had overlooked.

"Bowed tendon," he said, still petting her.

I looked down at her front legs, and sure enough, there it was, a bowed tendon. I couldn't believe it. Each of the three horses that I'd picked had something wrong with them. The things they had wrong with them weren't little things either. They were big things. Big things that I should have seen, but didn't.

"Come on," the old man smiled. "Let's go look at some of these others."

As we began walking back through the pens, I think the old man knew how bad I was feeling about my poor choices. He tried to make some small talk, but I didn't feel much like answering.

"Don't worry," he said finally. "The things you missed on those horses are the things that a lot of people would have missed."

It didn't help. As we continued along, he slowly began to explain what it takes to buy a horse wisely and where I had made my mistakes. He said that many first-time horse buyers make the same mistakes I had when looking to buy a horse. They buy the horse from the head down. In other words, they look for a horse that looks good to them. They look for a horse whose color catches their eye or whose physical build is impressive in one way or another. In some cases, it's the horse's personality that makes an impression. They see the good things about the horse, the obvious things. What they don't see or, in some cases, don't look for, are the bad things—the things that can tell you if the horse is going to be the one you want once you get it home.

The old man said that, unless he was looking for a certain type of horse or a horse that he would be using for a specific purpose, he always used the same method of elimination, if you will, to choose the ones he would ultimately buy. For instance, on that particular day, we were looking for three good saddle horses. It didn't necessarily matter how big they were, or what color, or what they looked like. All we wanted were good, sound horses with an even temperament. Knowing that, he proceeded to tell me how his process of elimination worked. With each horse that we looked at, instead of looking for its good points, he tried to find some kind of physical problem or a deficiency that would raise a red flag. The things that he looked for were things that I probably would have never even thought of, had he not mentioned them.

For instance, we stopped at one pen and he pointed out the horse's feet. At first, I didn't see anything different between that gelding's feet and any of the others that were there that day. That was, until he started to show me the difference.

"If you look real close at this horse's feet," he said, "you can see that they're pretty long, and they're chipped and split. That tells us that this horse hasn't had his feet trimmed in at least a month and probably longer. There also aren't any old nail holes in the hoof wall, which tells us that he hasn't had any shoes on in a while either. That makes me wonder when the last time was that he was ridden, if ever." He paused, turning his attention to the horse's mane and tail.

"If you look at his mane and tail," he continued, "you can see they're both pretty long. But even more interesting than that is the fact that the hair is stretched and broken in places. That tells us that he probably had some bad tangles or burrs that had to be combed or pulled out before they brought him here. If that's the case, that means that he hasn't been groomed in awhile, which also means he probably hasn't been handled in awhile. What do you think? Is he one that we should think about buying?"

"Probably not," I replied.

From there, we made our way to the rest of the pens, and he took a minute at each one to point out things that would concern him about each horse. At one pen, he noticed the deep outline of a halter on the horse's face, a sign that the horse had probably been wearing a halter for quite awhile before being brought to the auction. That, he said, could be a sign that the horse was hard to catch or even unbroke. Hard-to-catch and unbroken horses often are forced to wear their halters at all times. There were some horses with fresh scrapes and cuts on their foreheads, faces, and legs—a sign that the owner may have had trouble loading them in the trailer to bring them to the sale. There were horses with old rope burns on their fetlocks, a sign that they may have been hard to shoe. There were a couple of horses with quite a few brands on them, a sign that they'd had several different owners. With those horses, he pointed out, one had to wonder why they'd been sold so many times.

He showed me horses with things that didn't look right in other ways. Joint problems, bad scars on legs, eyes that didn't look clear, deformed hooves that, in some cases, were the result of founder and, in other cases, the result of a birth defect. In other words, he showed me how to look at the horse from the ground up. Instead of looking for the horse's good physical qualities, he showed me how to look for its bad ones. He told me that by looking for a horse's bad qualities and having an idea about what caused them, many times you can figure out what kind of training or medical problems you're likely to run into once you get the horse home. By eliminating the horses that aren't sound, either mentally or physically, it's easier to find a horse you can use and that will fit your particular needs.

By the time we had looked at all the horses, he had narrowed his choices down to about five or six. He waited until the sale started to make his decision on which ones to bid on. He decided by watching the way they were ridden into the sale ring. He observed how much pressure it took to turn them, stop them, and back them. He took note of what bit was being used on the horse and whether the rider was wearing spurs or not. If the rider was wearing spurs, he watched how the rider used them and how the horse reacted to them.

He processed all of this information within the first few minutes when the horse entered the arena, then made his decision on whether to bid on it. When he did decide to bid on a horse, he usually waited until the other people bidding on it were just about done before he jumped in. He told me that by entering the bidding late, many times you have a better chance of getting the horse you want for the price you want. Providing, of course, that somebody wasn't bidding the horse up. "Bidding up" is the term he used when people would bid on the horse with no intention of buying it, just so they could get the price of the animal as high as possible. It was usually a friend of the seller and, in some cases, the seller himself. That didn't seem to be the case, however, with the horses that the old man decided to bid on that day, and as a result, the prices he ended up paying were all very reasonable.

We went home that day having bought three nice horses. One was a mare and the other two were geldings. They weren't the prettiest horses I'd ever seen, but they were all very well trained and sound, which is all we were after to begin with.

"Remember," I recall the old man telling me, on our way home from the sale that day, "just because a horse is shiny doesn't necessarily mean he's going to be a good horse. The good ones, shiny or not, will show themselves to you. You just have to know what to look for."

It would be tough for me to guess how many horse auctions I've been to since that day, but the one thing I do know is that at each one I've kept the old man's advice in mind. I've always tried to buy the horses from the ground up. Some of the same rules apply, I've found, when buying horses from private individuals. You still want to give the horse you're buying a good look, but when buying from an individual, I've found that it also pays to take a couple of extra precautions.

For instance, some time ago I went to look at a horse that was advertised in the paper as being a "gentle 12-year-old grade quarter horse gelding. Kid broke and a good trail horse." At the time, I was buying horses to help fill a dude string, and from the ad, this one sounded like something that would fit right into the program. Not wanting to miss out on what could have been the perfect horse for our string, I called the number in the ad and made an appointment to go look at the horse. The fellow told me a little more about the gelding when I talked to him over the phone, and the things that he told me about him only seemed to confirm the fact that this was a horse that we needed to have. He did say, however, that the only time I could come to look at the horse was on Saturday afternoon at one o'clock. He told me not to come any sooner because nobody would be home and his dog wouldn't allow me on the place without someone from the family being there. I told him that wouldn't be a problem and that I'd see him on Saturday.

I arrived at the fellow's place about 1:15 and found the horse tied to a hitch rail in the yard, already saddled and bridled. As I got out of my truck and walked over to the horse, an older gentleman came out of the nearby barn and met me about halfway. He was followed by an old black-and-white dog that didn't look as though it was going to make it through the day. In fact, as the fellow and I introduced ourselves and continued on over to the horse, the dog fell down where it stood and immediately went to sleep.

"Well," the fellow said, when we got up next to the gelding, "like I told you over the phone, he's a real good horse. We've had him on the trails around here and up in the mountains, and the grandkids ride him a lot. In fact, they were out riding him just this morning. That's why he looks a little sweaty."

That was the first thing I'd noticed when I walked up. The horse had a great deal of dried sweat on his neck and chest, around the cinch line, on his back, and on his face, as if he had been ridden hard for a long time, then had been left there to stand and dry off.

"How long did they ride him?" I asked, running my hand over the horse's chest to see if he was still warm, which he was.

"Oh," he replied, "I guess about an hour or so. Not very long. In fact, they all just left a little while ago."

"I see," I nodded. "Would you mind showing me how he works?"

"Normally I'd be happy to," he said, reaching around and squeezing his lower back with his hand, "but my dang back has been acting up lately, and I'm afraid I wouldn't even be able to get in the saddle. You can go ahead and ride him though, if you want."

I was getting a very strange feeling about this situation. I didn't know exactly why, but it had something to do with the fact that what the man had told me over the phone a few days before and what was happening that day were two completely different things. For instance, he'd told me that nobody was going to be home until one o'clock that afternoon and that if I arrived before that, his dog would probably attack me. What he was telling me to my face was that someone had been there all morning and, in fact, had been riding the horse I'd come to see. The dog that would attack me if I showed up early was not only sound asleep in the yard but was so old that it would probably be lucky even to wake up. These were definitely warning signs that I should have paid attention to before I got on the horse, but unfortunately, I didn't.

I adjusted the stirrups, climbed in the saddle, and urged the horse forward. He moved into a nice walk, and we started down the driveway that led past the barn and into an open field. While going past the side of the barn, I happened to look down and notice that the ground was freshly torn up with hoof prints. The hoof prints were in a circle, similar in size and appearance to a longeing circle. Moving past the circle, we made our way out into the field where I asked the horse to stop, back, and turn, all of which he did with little hesitation. I worked the horse in a walk for about ten minutes with no trouble, before I asked him to move into a trot. That was where I made my mistake and where my concerns about the situation were confirmed.

The horse responded by moving into a slow trot, which quickly turned into a fast trot. Before I could ask him to slow down, he pinned his ears back and broke into a lope for about three strides, then completely blew the cork. He took off bucking like his life depended on it, and within about four or five jumps, I found myself flying through the air. Had it not been for gravity, I expect I wouldn't have landed as hard as I did, but as it was, it was one of those landings that kind of makes a person wish he'd chosen a different profession in life, something a little less detrimental to one's health. Perhaps a tennis shoe inspector or something along those lines.

The fellow took his time getting out to me, and as the horse bucked, squealed, and snorted his way around the field and back up to the barn, he said simply, "I've never seen him do that before," as if it were actually the truth. I brushed my pants off, found my hat, and made my way back to my truck. The fellow followed me, the whole time telling me how good a horse the gelding normally was and that I should give him another try. All I could do, however, was thank the man for his time, climb in my truck and drive away, the whole time feeling like I'd been taken advantage of. At any rate, it was an experience that helped me change the way I look at buying horses from private individuals.

There were two things in particular that I decided to change because of what happened that day. The first change was in the time

I arrive to see a horse that I'm interested in. If the owner wants me there at a certain time, I usually find myself arriving half an hour to forty-five minutes early. I'm always very apologetic for arriving early, but at the same time, I'm always interested in what's going on with the horse when I do arrive. On one occasion, a woman selling a horse had assured me over the phone that her horse was very easy to catch. I arrived a half-hour early to see her in the corral with a halter in one hand, a grain bucket in the other, and the horse doing everything in its power to stay away from her.

On another occasion, an owner told me that his horse was dog gentle and absolutely kid broke. A half-hour before I was supposed to show up, he had the horse in the round pen and was longeing him at a lope. The horse was sweaty enough that he'd probably been loping for quite a while before I got there, and he had enough energy left over that he could have loped for quite a while longer. The whole time he was being longed he was also snorting and shaking his head, as well as kicking and bucking. Not exactly my idea of "dog gentle."

By accidentally arriving early when looking to buy a horse, I've seen supposedly quiet and gentle horses that kicked when you walked behind them, bit or bloated when you tried to cinch them, pulled back when you tried to tie them, and threw their heads when you tried to bridle them. In one case, I even walked in on a fellow as he was injecting the horse he wanted to sell me with a sedative.

Now there are some people who think that showing up early to an appointment is the ultimate in being rude. Maybe they're right. But when it comes right down to it, if somebody is trying to misrepresent a horse that they're trying to sell, then, in my opinion, they're the ones being rude. If the person selling the horse isn't trying to hide anything and truly wants to sell the horse, it's been my experience that he or she usually isn't put out by the buyer showing up a little early. It's usually the folks trying to pull a fast one who get upset when you show up before you're supposed to.

When I'm looking to buy from an individual, there's another thing I do that's often a great deal of help when considering the horse. I simply have either the owner or someone who knows the horse demonstrate how the horse works. If neither the owner nor anyone else wants to ride the horse, then there's a pretty good chance that I don't either. By insisting that someone demonstrate the animal, I completely eliminate the chances of becoming injured if the horse isn't what the seller claims. I also get the opportunity to see how well the horse is trained, what cues are being used, and how well it responds to them. The folks who are selling a good horse, as a rule, will not only be happy to demonstrate the animal, but will usually go out of their way to show off all of the animal's good qualities. The folks who are selling a bad horse, as a rule, would rather not demonstrate the animal at all.

Unfortunately, I've found that even after taking all of these precautions, there is still no guarantee that the horse you end up buying is going to be the horse you want. There are some horse traders and sellers out there who will say and do anything to get you to buy their horses, including misrepresenting an animal's background and lineage by switching registration papers with another horse that has a similar color and markings and, in some cases, telling outright lies about the horse's health or state of soundness.

I remember two horses in particular that I helped purchase, that had been deliberately misrepresented by their sellers. In one instance, a client of mine had been looking to buy a young horse that she could train for showing in western pleasure classes. She had been looking for about three weeks before she finally found one that she thought might work. The horse was a young mare, just under four years old, that she'd found through a newspaper ad. She called the number in the ad and talked to the seller on several occasions before finally deciding to go have a look at the horse. When she did, she called me to ask if I'd be willing to go along, which I happily agreed to do.

When we arrived at the place where the horse was kept, we found the mare alone in a small back pasture. She apparently had just been fed because she was contentedly eating from a small pile of alfalfa hay. We had no sooner walked up to the pasture fence than the seller, a woman in her mid-twenties, came walking up. She was very pleasant and willing to answer any and all of our questions pertaining to the mare. After a brief conversation, she went into the pasture and easily caught and haltered the mare, then brought her out and tied her to a nearby trailer. From inside the tack compartment, the woman brought out her saddle and bridle and quietly went about the business of tacking the mare up. It was clear that the horse wasn't at all bothered by the sound and feel of the heavy saddle being tossed up on her back or having the cinch tightened around her. She also accepted the bit without hesitation and stood perfectly still while the woman mounted up.

The woman told us that she hadn't had much time to work with the mare and, in fact, she had only had her under saddle for about two months. She also told us that the mare seemed to be a very fast and willing learner. She took the mare out in the pasture and walked, trotted, and loped her. She did some sliding stops and spins and backed her with very little effort. She rode the horse for about twenty minutes and the mare didn't seem to have any trouble understanding or responding to the cues that the woman was giving. The horse seemed to be everything that my client was looking for. She was well-bred, well-mannered, well-started, and guaranteed sound by the seller.

It seemed clear to me that we would have very little trouble turning the mare into the pleasure horse that my client wanted. After a brief discussion between myself and my client pertaining to the mare's good points and bad points, she made the decision to go ahead and buy her. Two days later the mare was delivered to the stable where my client boarded her horses, and it was only after the horse entered the pen where she was to be kept that a major problem became apparent.

As soon as the mare was turned loose in the pen, she calmly walked over to the nearest fence post, put her top teeth on it, and sucked. Much to my client's dismay, and mine, we had been duped into buying a "wind sucker," a horse with the dangerous, annoying, and nearly incurable habit of sucking air into its stomach through its mouth.

It's a habit that is normally unmistakably apparent because the horse will go to anything sticking up out of the ground, put its top teeth on it, and suck wind. However, because of the way the woman had presented this mare to us, the mare never had the opportunity to show us the problem. When we arrived to look at the mare, she was in a back pasture that was fenced with barbed wire, one of the only fences that's difficult for a horse to use to suck wind. The mare had also recently been fed, which is another thing that will temporarily stop a horse from sucking. There was nothing for the mare to get her teeth on when she was tied to the trailer, so she couldn't suck then, and she obviously couldn't do it while she was being ridden, so she didn't even try.

Wind sucking is one of those things that if you don't see the horse doing it, you just assume that it doesn't. The woman selling the mare knew that, and she also knew that if we'd seen the problem we probably wouldn't have purchased the horse. By the same token, I'm sure she knew that if we didn't see it, we probably wouldn't ask if the mare had that problem. As a result, the woman had successfully misrepresented the mare by intentionally not telling us that she was a wind sucker, and we had successfully opened ourselves up to be taken by not asking if she was. That was a mistake that I have not, and will not, make again.

As bad as it is to have someone misrepresent a horse to you, there is one type of horse seller that, in my opinion, is the lowest form of life there is. That's the person who deliberately and blatantly lies to you while trying to sell you a horse. This is the type of person who will tell you absolutely anything to make the sale, including the cardinal sin of horse trading—guaranteeing a horse sound when the seller knows it's lame. I had the misfortune of running into such a person awhile back, and I don't mind telling you, the experience leaves a bad taste in my mouth to this day.

I'd been asked by a friend of mine, Sandy Payne, to have a look at a horse that she was thinking about buying. The person selling the horse was relatively new to the area and sold and worked with horses as a hobby, more or less. His real occupation was as a cook in a coffee shop that he owned with his wife. The fellow, as I understood it, had been selling horses for about a year, and the whispering among the horse people in the area was that he had been selling unsound horses to first-time horse buyers, then refusing to take the horses back, even though he had guaranteed the animals sound prior to the sale. Of course, all of this talk, as far as I knew, was just that—talk. I had no firsthand knowledge of anything like that actually occurring, so when Sandy asked me to go look at the horse she was thinking of buying, I did so with an open mind.

I have to admit, I was quite impressed as I pulled into the yard of the fellow's horse operation that evening. The place was very clean and tidy, with the barn and rough-cedar fences being brand new. Sandy and the owner of the place, Bill, were both inside the barn grooming the horse when I arrived.

"Well," Sandy said with a smile, as I walked through the door, "here he is. What do you think?"

She was referring to the massive gelding standing tied in the middle of the barn alley. He stood about sixteen hands high and had to weigh at least 1,300 pounds. He was kind of a chestnut color, with a flaxen mane and tail, heavily muscled and well proportioned.

"He's pretty fancy," I replied. "How old is he?"

"He just turned three," Bill said with a big smile, as he came over and introduced himself. "He's been shown in halter for the last two years, but a couple of months ago we started him under saddle. He's doing real good, too." He paused, walking over to a wall that was full of saddles. "I'll get him saddled up and show you how he works. I think he's going to make a real good trail horse. In fact, we've had him out on the trails six or seven times now, and each time we go out he just seems to get better."

With that, he saddled the gelding, grabbed a nylon longe line, and took him out to a nearby round pen. After snapping the line on the gelding's halter, he stepped back a few paces and gave the horse a verbal command to walk, to which the horse responded immediately. After walking one full circle, he told the horse to trot, and again the horse responded. However, he'd only trotted about ten feet when he suddenly started to limp on his right rear leg.

"He looks a little off," I said, as the gelding trotted past me.

"He sure does," Bill said. He stopped the horse, walked up, and picked up the gelding's right front foot. "He probably just stepped on a stone."

"Has he ever been lame before?" I asked.

"No," Bill replied. "I'm sure he just stepped on a stone or something. Don't worry, I'll guarantee him sound. I wouldn't sell a lame horse."

Having said that, Bill went back to longeing the gelding for a little while longer, before taking him down to the arena. Once in the arena, he bridled the horse, got on, and began working him. It was clear that the gelding was pretty green. He was sluggish in responding to the cues that Bill gave him, and at times he even acted a little sleepy. Bill rode the horse for about half an hour, which was more than ample time for me to get a good look at him. Having watched the gelding work, I came to the conclusion that he was probably a fairly good horse, and even though he was green, he had a good enough start on him that the rest of his training should go relatively smooth.

About an hour later, after the horse had been put up for the night, Bill, Sandy, Bill's wife, and I sat and visited in front of the barn. Bill went on and on about all the young gelding's attributes, as well as those of other horses he owned. He also took the time, once again, to make it known that he guaranteed the gelding sound and, in fact, would do so for thirty days after the sale. Sandy had been looking for a horse to buy for the better part of two months, and she appeared to have decided upon this gelding as the one she wanted. The fact that Bill was willing to guarantee the horse for thirty days appeared to be the final selling point for her, and while I was there that evening, she made a verbal commitment to buy him. I made a point to mention that even though Bill was guaranteeing the horse, I felt the sale should be contingent upon the horse passing a pre-sale vet check, and both Bill and Sandy agreed that would be a good idea.

Later that evening, after I'd left, Bill suddenly remembered that he'd had the gelding vet checked only one month earlier, and the horse had, at that time, gotten a clean bill of health. He told Sandy that because the horse had just been checked, it would be a waste of money to have him checked again, and besides, if the horse happened to come up lame within thirty days, he'd give her money back anyway. Sandy gave the matter some thought and ultimately decided to save herself the extra cost by taking Bill at his word, and bypassed having a vet check done.

Two weeks after Sandy had given Bill a $5,000 cashier's check for the horse, she was out riding him on the trail when he suddenly came up terribly lame on his right rear leg. The gelding was so lame that Sandy couldn't continue to ride him and she ended up having to walk him back to the barn. Once back at the barn, she immediately called the vet and had him come out to have a look at the gelding. The vet gave him a thorough examination and, after careful deliberation, came to the conclusion that the horse was suffering from the initial stages of an incurable, congenital ligament disease. He stressed that, while the disease was incurable, it could be treated through an inexpensive surgery.

Sandy was beside herself and, in a panic, she called me, wondering what to do. I told her not to worry because Bill had guaranteed the horse sound for thirty days and she'd only had him for two weeks. I suggested getting in touch with Bill and explaining what was wrong with the horse. Not only had the animal come up lame within the thirty-day period that he'd guaranteed him for, but according to the vet, the problem had existed in the horse since birth. There was no question that the horse was unsound when Sandy bought him, whether Bill was aware of the problem or not. Surely he would honor his guarantee, take the horse back, and refund Sandy's money.

I was assuming, of course, that Bill was an honorable man and that when he gave his word, he intended to keep it. Unfortunately, that wasn't the case. As soon as Sandy told him what the problem was, Bill became very belligerent, claiming that the reason the horse became lame was that Sandy had put him away hot after riding him, which was simply untrue. He also said that while he did guarantee the horse sound, he only guaranteed him sound on the day of the purchase, not after.

I had never heard of such a thing. Not only was Bill not standing up to his agreement, but he was flat-out lying about the fact that he even made an agreement. This type of behavior was something that I wasn't accustomed to. I was used to dealing with people like my good friend Dwight Thorson, who, whenever he sells a horse, simply tells the buyer, "If you don't like him, you don't own him," and then stands behind his word. Bill, on the other hand, was a whole different breed. He was the type of fellow who gave his word as part of making a sale—it didn't mean anything, and he had no intention of keeping it. That was how he did business, and if you believed what he was saying, then shame on you for being taken. It certainly wasn't his fault if you were stupid enough to believe him. In fact, in Sandy's case, Bill actually felt that he was the one who was being wronged, and he couldn't understand why people who heard about his refusal to take the horse back got so upset with him.

The good part of this story is that Sandy refused to let the matter be, and eventually she was able to force Bill to not only take the horse back, but also to give her a replacement horse. Bill had surgery done on the gelding to repair the ligament problem and took him to a major horse sale. However, the wound from the surgery hadn't healed very well and had left a gaping hole in the gelding's leg. Bill, of course, didn't want any prospective buyers to know that the gelding had ever been operated on, so he told people who were looking at the horse that the wound was a puncture wound that he'd gotten while coming out of a trailer, and he somehow was able to acquire a vet report to that effect.

A few days after the sale, I was happy to hear that Bill had been caught misrepresenting the horse, and had not only been banned from that sale for life, but was also being investigated on charges of fraud. I'd been discussing the situation with my buddy Marlin Flowers, who summed it up best when he said, "Guys like that always ride tall in the saddle, right up until their blister breaks."

Unfortunately, being caught usually only serves to slow people like Bill down. It seldom, if ever, stops them. It's for that reason I always suggest to people who are buying a horse, that they be very leery of taking the seller at his word. Make sure to get all the terms of the sale in writing, especially if you don't know the people you're buying from. If they don't want to put the terms in writing, then you probably don't need that particular horse very badly. After all, you may find that you're dealing with Bill or someone like him. Of course, having the terms in writing still won't stop people from cheating you if they're of a mind to do so, but it will certainly help you if you're forced to take the matter to court.

People often ask me what the secret is to buying a good horse, and how to avoid being taken by folks like Bill. The answer I most commonly give is to look at buying a horse like you would look at buying a used car. It's been my experience that when folks are out car shopping, they're usually looking for some very specific things. They look for quality, dependability, and value—the very same features most people look for when buying horses. The biggest difference is that when people are buying a car, the make and model are often a factor in the decision, but the color seldom is. If the car seems to have the qualities they're looking for, the color doesn't matter. When buying horses, people look for all the desirable qualities, but may ultimately make their final decision based on the animal's color. On many occasions, I've seen someone buy a lesser-quality horse because it's of a more desirable color, then kick themselves after they get the animal home because it isn't what they'd hoped it would be.

A long time ago, the old man taught me that the best way to buy a good horse is to eliminate all the bad ones. Buy the horse for what it is, not what it looks like. Look at the horse from the ground up, not from the head down. He taught me to know exactly what I was looking for, even before I started looking, then not to stop until I found it. The most important thing he taught me, though, is that if I'm set on buying the right color, chances are, I won't end up with the right horse. By the same token, if I buy the right horse, I probably won't get the right color.

"The thing you might want to keep in mind," I recall him telling me, "is that when it gets right down to it, it's usually better to have the best horse in the barn, not the prettiest."

It was a simple piece of advice from one horseperson to another, and in my opinion, it's the difference between buying a good horse and buying one that's just good to look at. For my money, I think I'd rather have the former. I'll leave the latter for someone else.

PART THREE

Making a Good One

6

Babies

I HATED DAYS like this. It was cold and damp with a drizzle that was just heavy enough to soak you from head to foot if you were out in it for more than a few minutes. I'd been making a point to get to work early the last couple of days, and the rotten weather wasn't making it any easier. Riding a bike in weather like that was like taking a shower with all your clothes on. At any rate, I finally did get to work, and as I entered the tack room, I was delighted to see that the old man had a fire going in the old potbellied stove. I stood in front of the stove for a short time, trying to shake off the chill, when I heard the old man call from inside the foaling stall that was attached to the tack room.

"I'm going to need your help in here," he said rather bluntly.

I quickly went over to the stall door and found the old man inside. He was kneeling down behind a mare that we'd been waiting to foal for the last two weeks. She was laying flat on her right side and was wringing wet with sweat.

"The colt's upside down," he said, out of breath, as I made my way around to him. "She can't get him out and I can't pull him myself. He's too big. You grab that foot, I'll grab this one, and when she starts pushing, we'll start pulling."

This was the reason I'd been trying to get to work early for the past couple of days. We knew that this mare was pretty close to having her baby, and I'd been hoping that I'd come in one morning, and there it'd be. I never expected that I would see the birth and certainly never thought I'd be helping with it. But there I was, kneeling next to the old man, holding on to one of the baby's front feet, which were the only things sticking out of the mare.

"Get ready," the old man said, still out of breath. "Here she goes."

Just then, the mare's whole body began to shake.

"Pull!" the old man said, half shouting.

Together, the old man and I pulled with everything we had. The little bit of extra muscle that I provided must have been all the mare needed, because as she pushed and we pulled, the baby's nose and eyes began to appear.

"Keep pulling," the old man grunted. "We need to get past the shoulder."

We pulled for a few seconds longer, but the mare stopped pushing.

"Okay," the old man puffed, as we both stopped pulling. "Take a break, but get ready. We need to get him on this next go."

There was a sense of urgency in his voice. It was hard to say how long he'd been working on getting the colt out, but by the sweat that was rolling off both him and the mare, I would guess it had probably been quite a while. I had never seen the old man flustered before, but this situation seemed to have him that way, and I wasn't really sure why. I'd never been involved in a horse's birth before, so I didn't know if what we were going through was normal or not. The fact that we could have lost the colt, and possibly even the mare because of the trouble she was having, never even crossed my mind.

"Here we go," the old man said.

Once again, the mare's body began to shake, and once again we began to pull. I remember closing my eyes, gritting my teeth, and pulling for all I was worth. I remember pulling so hard that I could feel the strain in my shoulders and back, and it felt like we were going to turn the mare inside out before we'd get that darn baby to move. I was just beginning to think that we weren't going to get it done, when suddenly the baby moved. It wasn't just a little move either. It was a big move. So big, in fact, that I lost my balance and fell over backwards, landing squarely in a small pile of fresh manure. It didn't matter though, because when I looked up, I could see that the baby was over halfway out, and with one more pull from the old man, who unlike me was still holding on to the colt, it came the rest of the way.

As soon as the baby was out, the old man began tearing the thin sack that the baby came in, to expose the little fellow's wet skin.

"Grab those rags," he said, still puffing pretty hard. "We need to get him dried off."

Lying in a small pile off in the corner of the stall were three or four old bath towels. I quickly went over, picked up the pile, and brought them back to the old man. It was only then that I noticed the entire stall was full of steam. This was due, of course, to the fact that the air in the stall was considerably colder than the sweat coming off the old man and the mare, as well as the moisture on the baby's wet skin.

"Here," he said, taking one of the towels and rubbing the baby with it. "Get him as dry as you can on this side, then we'll turn him over and do the other side. I need to check on the mare."

With that, he handed me the towel, and leaving me with the baby, he went immediately over to the mare. That was the first opportunity I had to get a good look at the colt, and I don't mind saying, I wasn't impressed with what I saw. He had long, spindly legs attached to a thin, drawn-up body. His ears were flopped backwards on top of what seemed like an enormous head, and they looked deformed. His feet were white and soft and looked as though they had a sort of toe growing off the end of them, and they certainly had very little appearance of the healthy hoof that he would need in the future. His lips and muzzle seemed to be covered with thousands of curly whiskers, similar to those of a ninety-four-year-old man who hadn't shaved in a couple of weeks. On top of all that, he was soaking wet, which made him look more like a refugee from a "Goats on Skis" water show extravaganza than a baby horse.

As a matter of fact, as I knelt there toweling off this pathetic-looking creature, the only positive thing that I could see about him was his coloring. He was a very uniquely marked paint horse, dark brown or black, with a cream-colored, almost white, mane and tail. He had a large blaze on his face and four white stockings that went nearly to his knees. I couldn't help but think that if it wasn't for the fact that he looked so physically deformed, his coloring would probably make him a very attractive horse when he grew up.

"You aren't going to break him," the old man said, from his position next to the mare. Evidently, I either wasn't pressing hard enough with the towel or else I wasn't going fast enough. At any rate, I got the message and began to do both.

About that time the mare let out a soft nicker, to which the baby responded with one of his own. This caused the mare, although exhausted, to climb to her feet and slowly turn toward the colt. By standing up, she broke the baby's umbilical cord and separated the two for the first time.

"Okay," the old man said, still standing by the mare, "she's going to want to try to get him to stand up. Just keep on doing what you're doing, but keep an eye on her so she doesn't accidentally step on you. I'm going to get a halter."

The old man went into the tack room and quickly returned with an adult-sized halter, which I assumed he was going to put on the mare. Much to my surprise, however, he brought the halter over to the baby.

"Isn't that going to be too big?" I questioned, surprised that he would try to put something that large on the baby's head. After all, the halter was almost as big as the baby. The old man just smiled.

"I'll show you a little trick," he replied, as he turned the halter upside down and slipped the nose band over the baby's head. He moved the nose piece clear down to the base of the colt's neck, then took the strap that would normally go behind an adult horse's ears, and slid it under the baby's girth. "There," he grunted, as he half-lifted the colt, pushing the strap through at the same time. "Grab ahold of that and buckle it on that side."

I did what he said, pulling the strap under the colt and buckling it in place. It was only then that I could see what it was he was doing. By inverting an adult-sized halter and putting it on the colt the way he did, he had devised a sort of harness for the baby. The nose piece of the halter was around the base of the baby's neck, the buckled strap was around the baby's girth, and the strap that would normally run under the adult's jaw now ran between the two, along the colt's back. This made a sort of handle that we could use to help pick the baby up and assist him in getting to his feet, if needed.

We had no sooner gotten the halter in place than the mare came over and started to smell and lick the baby. She also began to nudge him gently with her front feet, and after a while, because he apparently wasn't responding the way she thought he should, she began to kick him. When that didn't work, she started to step lightly on his hip and flank area, and finally she resorted to nipping at him in the same places.

"Isn't she going to hurt him?" I asked, a little worried about what I was seeing. The old man smiled, picked up one of the towels and vigorously rubbed the colt's neck, head, and face.

"I think she knows what she's doing," he commented.

She must have, because no sooner had he said that than the colt began to stir. He scooted himself around a little, apparently trying to get to his feet, but he only fell back down each time he started making any progress. It took several struggling attempts on the colt's part and some assistance from the old man and myself by lifting on the halter, but after a while he finally did stand up. Once he was on his feet, he slowly made his way to the mare's flank, apparently looking for some breakfast, and the old man and I were with him every step

of the way. In fact, once he got to his destination, it was the old man who directed his mouth to his mother's udder and got him nursing.

"Do we leave them alone now?" I asked.

"We could," the old man replied, "but I think it'll be better for the colt if we don't. We'll let him eat for a while, then we'll start on his training."

"Training?" I asked, somewhat surprised. "What kind of training?"

"I'll show you in a little bit," he said, picking the towels up out of the straw that covered the stall floor. "In the meantime, why don't you go on out and get your chores done? When you're finished, come on back and we'll get started."

I got my chores done just as quickly as I possibly could and returned to the stall. I was surprised at what I saw. Not only had the stall been tidied up, but the mare was up and eating, and the ugly little deformed-looking colt that I had left earlier now looked a whole lot better. Oh, he was still skinny, and his legs still appeared a whole lot longer than they should, but otherwise he was starting to look a lot more like a normal colt. His ears were standing up and no longer looked deformed. He was completely dried off, which caused his hair to look real soft and fluffy and almost completely eliminated the drawn-up look that he'd had earlier. Even his hooves were starting to look more normal, with the toe-looking thing on the end of them starting to wear off. Overall, he was really a pretty nice looking colt.

Once I got back, the old man began to show me how to work with the colt. He started by showing me what he called the most important thing a colt should know—how to gain trust and respect for people and, at the same time, how to give to pressure. He explained that by teaching the colt how to give to pressure now instead of later, we could help speed up his future training. He would pick up things like leading, tying, and having his feet handled quicker and easier, and it would also transfer to the things he would be learning later in life, like responding to leg and hand cues. The old man's method for doing this was so simple that it was hard for me to believe that it could teach the colt anything at all. But it didn't take me long to understand the thinking behind it.

With the colt awake but still lying down, the old man quietly walked over and encouraged the colt to stand up using a technique much like the colt's mother had. He started by bumping the colt lightly in the hip with the toe of his boot. When that didn't work, he bent down and began lightly pinching him on the hip and flank. That did the trick. The baby, still very wobbly, climbed to his feet and tried to walk off a little ways. Before he could even take two steps, however, the old man gently wrapped his arms around him, while making sure the colt was always in plain sight of his mother. One arm went around the colt's chest, the other around his back legs. The baby began to fight, squirming and kicking as best he could.

The old man held his arms in one spot, neither tightening nor loosening his grip, and remained in that position until the colt began to quit fighting. As soon as the colt showed signs of giving up, the old man ever so slightly released his grip. He let the colt rest for a few seconds, then once again tightened his grip. The colt squirmed a bit, but stopped almost immediately. The old man repeated this several times before letting the colt loose and walking him over to his mother, using the halter that the colt was still wearing to assist him. He allowed the colt to nurse, while both he and I went into the tack room. After letting the colt nurse for about five minutes, we went back in and he started all over. Surprisingly enough, the colt didn't fight at all.

Seeing that the colt wasn't fighting, the old man told me that he had a good jump on the first part of the lesson, learning to give to pressure. He told me that the colt was ready for the second part of the lesson—learning to trust and respect people. He said that the best way he'd found to accomplish that was by doing one simple thing. That one thing, strange as it may sound, was picking the colt up off the ground.

He said that by picking the colt up, we'd be reinforcing the fact that he should give to pressure and, at the same time, we'd be giving him the impression that it would do no good to fight with us because we were bigger and stronger. So strong that we could pick him right up off the ground any time we wanted to. The fact that he was still small and weak only served to help our case because if the colt did try to fight, he could only do so for a short time before he'd play out. If done properly, the old man told me, the colt would begin to gain a tremendous amount of respect for the person doing the lifting. He'd learn that it doesn't pay to fight because the person has what appeared to be supernatural strength. At the same time, by lifting the colt in a way that put the least amount of mental stress on him, he wouldn't be put in a position where he felt he had to defend himself, thereby allowing the colt to start developing the trust in us that he'd need to have in the future.

After explaining all this, the old man went over to the colt and maneuvered him around so that the colt's side was facing the mare. He reached down and gently put his arms around the colt in the same manner that he had for the last half-hour. The colt was very quiet and appeared comfortable with the old man. Still facing the mare, the old man ever so slowly and carefully began to pick the colt up off the ground. The colt squirmed and fought, but that didn't stop the old man from standing up with him in his arms, and soon enough the colt quit. As soon as the colt quieted down, the old man gently put him back on the ground for a few seconds, let him stand, then picked him up again. This went on for about ten minutes, the old man having picked the colt up ten or fifteen times within that period. After that, he put the colt down, walked him over to his mother, and let him nurse. After about five minutes, he once again approached the colt and gently picked him up. This time the baby hardly fought at all, and after picking him up and setting him down about half a dozen times, the old man turned the baby loose.

"What we're going to want to do," the old man said after turning the baby loose, "is work with him like this on both sides every day for about the next week. If we do, the chances are real good that for the rest of his life he'll have it in his head that we can control him and even pick him up any time we want. That'll give us an advantage over him as he gets older. He'll always want to try and stay on our good side and do what we ask of him, because he'll remember that we have this superhuman strength. The last thing he's going to want is for us to get mad at him because he's been bad and come over and pick him up."

It was an interesting concept, one that I had never heard of before or since. It was, however, one that certainly appeared to work with that particular colt. The old man owned him until he was two years old, and during that time, I noticed the colt was always very quiet, trusting, and willing whenever he was learning new things. He was especially willing when it came to things like accepting a saddle for the first time, having his feet handled, and being loaded in a trailer. Not only that, but right from the start he seemed to have a tremendous amount of respect, not just for the old man, but for anyone he came in contact with, including men, women, and children. He never nipped at or bit anyone that I knew of, and he never rubbed his head on people like most colts do. I noticed that he was always respectful of his handlers. When being led, he always kept at least two feet away from the person leading him, even if something happened to scare him. He never rushed through gates or ran people over when going through them, like many colts do, and he was one of the easiest colts to catch that I've ever seen.

I never forgot the results the old man seemed to get with that colt, using his slightly unconventional training technique. In fact, over the years, I've even had the opportunity to use the technique on a couple of occasions, with many of the same long-term results. I must admit, however, that watching the old man perform the technique and trying to perform it myself were two completely different things. He made it look easy, as he did anytime he worked with horses. On the other hand, I wasn't quite as graceful. I found that even small, weak babies can put up quite a struggle, and they often ended up kicking me in places where I didn't care to be kicked. I've also found that if they should happen to get loose from you, or you release the pressure before they quit struggling, you can teach them just the opposite of what you're trying to. They'll learn that the best way to get themselves free of any kind of pressure is to fight it. That can obviously result in quite a problem as they get older. Horses that learn how to fight pressure when they're babies are the same ones that pull back when tied, are hard to catch, hard to shoe, hard to stop and turn, don't lead very well, and are generally misbehaved when they get older.

Most people who work with babies on a regular basis know all too well how important it is to get a good start on them. They also know how to avoid making mistakes that could possibly come back to haunt them (and the horse) in the future. The old man was one of those people. His philosophy, and I'm sure the key to his success when it came to working with babies, was based on remembering one simple thing. He always treated babies like babies. He explained to me once that the biggest mistake most people make when they work with babies is that they treat babies the same way they treat adult horses. They figure that because a baby horse is still a horse, all the same rules of training should apply.

"The reason that's a mistake," I remember him telling me, "is because baby horses don't learn the same way adults do. Horses are a lot like people in that respect. A colt's understanding of the world isn't as well developed as, say, its mother's, so he'll rely on his mother to teach him about the world. If his mother isn't around, the baby has to rely on his instincts to help him survive."

He went on to explain that if you're working with a colt and he starts fighting what you're doing, chances are it's because he doesn't understand it. If he doesn't understand it, naturally it's going to frighten him and his instincts are going to kick in. His instincts tell him either to get away or defend himself. These actions on the colt's part are often mistaken by the inexperienced handler as the colt being belligerent or mean, and so the handler responds by reprimanding him for unacceptable behavior. Now, the problem here is that if the handler reprimands him for the way he is responding, the colt is probably going to become more frightened, which will make him want to fight even more. Instead of making the behavior better, it actually gets worse.

In my experience, this response on the colt's part can be almost completely eliminated if the handler simply understands the colt's instincts—why he acts and reacts the way he does. By understanding and remembering not to get in any kind of hurry when working with a young horse, it becomes easier to form a plan for his training. It also makes a big difference as to the kind of horse you ultimately end up with. I recall one little horse in particular that, had we not taken the time to look at things from his point of view, could have ended up being considered a troublemaker. In reality, his only problem was that he was a baby. Not only that, but he was a baby that had lived in the wild and had absolutely no idea of how to respond to, or live with, people.

I was given that three-month-old colt several years ago by a friend of mine, Steve Wilson, who runs one of the biggest and best-run liveries in the state of Colorado. The colt had been born to one of Steve's older mares shortly after she had been turned out on winter pasture. It had come as a complete surprise because, as far as Steve knew, the old mare hadn't been anywhere near a stallion in years. At any rate, Steve was concerned that neither the colt nor the mare would be strong enough to make it through the harsh winter months ahead, running loose on the open pasture. He told me that if I'd be willing to board them both for the winter, he'd give me the colt. Not one to ever turn down a free horse, I happily agreed.

Little did I know when Steve jumped the pair out of his trailer during one of the worst snowstorms of the year, that the spooky little colt running at the mare's side would end up being one of the finest horses I've ever come across. I should point out, however, that even though that was the end result, it certainly wasn't the way our relationship started. In fact, when my wife Wendy and I went out to start working with the colt for the first time about a week after he'd been dropped off, what we found was the complete opposite. The colt was not only still spooky concerning most things in general, but he also had no desire whatsoever to become friendly with anything that walked on two legs. I'm sure that was because even though we had been feeding and watering the colt and his mother, we still looked like predators, something he should stay away from. At any rate, we knew that the longer we waited to start his handling and training, the worse his attitude was likely to get.

The biggest problem we were up against was the fact that, unlike babies that are handled from birth, this colt was completely unfamiliar with humans and how we do things. He'd been born, and lived for the first three months of his life in a 2,500-acre pasture with no contact with humans at all. Even though his mother was a domesticated horse and had no fear of people, he was a wild horse that had been forced to use his instincts to help him survive. Being caught and handled went against everything he'd learned. In the pasture he had learned that when something frightened him, all he needed to do to make himself safe was to run away from it. If he couldn't get away, he would panic and fight.

In order for this colt to become comfortable being handled, we were going to have to do two things. First, we were going to have to get him over his fear of people. We were going to have to prove to him that he could trust and rely on us and that we weren't going to hurt him. The second thing we were going to have to do, and in some respects the most important, was to show him how to give to pressure. In other words, how not to fight against us. If we could get those two things accomplished, the chances of us ending up with a pretty good horse when it was all said and done would improve greatly. But first we had to get him caught. That, it turned out, was the biggest hurdle we had to overcome.

Catching the colt was difficult because the corral the colt and mare were in was fairly big, measuring about sixty feet by 100 feet, with no access to any kind of smaller enclosures nearby. At the time, we were unable to find any portable panels to build a smaller catch pen inside the large corral. As a result, we were forced to devise a way of catching the colt in the wide-open pen. We decided that we needed to limit the area that the two could move around in, particularly the mare. We wanted to limit the mare's movement because the colt would instinctively follow her wherever she went. If we could keep her in one spot, the colt wouldn't be quite as likely to wander away or run off.

Keeping that in mind, the first thing Wendy and I did before trying to work with the colt was catch his mother and tie her in a corner of the corral. We tied her to the very top rail so if the colt decided to run under her neck as we attempted to catch him he wouldn't get hung up in her rope. We also tied her so that her head was facing the corner, and we did this for a specific reason that will become evident in a minute. The mare was quiet and cooperative as we tied her and she seemed very content just to stand patiently exactly where we'd placed her. Had she acted mean, agitated, or upset, we would have had to turn her loose and try plan B, which we hadn't even thought of yet. I guess it was lucky we didn't have to use it.

At any rate, we quickly found that as quiet as the mare was, the colt didn't care to have anything to do with us and, in fact, even left his mother and headed for the other end of the corral. Wendy and I walked out to the colt and slowly started herding him back in the general direction of his mother. He obliged us by making a beeline back to her. Looking for some comfort, he began to nurse as soon as he reached her. Wendy and I continued to make our way slowly toward the pair, stopping every once in a while so as not to frighten the colt unnecessarily. Wendy was approaching from the left side of the mare, which was the side the colt was on, and I was approaching from the right. By standing next to the mare, with Wendy between her and the fence on one side and me between her and the fence on the other, we were effectively putting the colt in a tiny triangular catch pen with the fence making up two sides of the triangle, Wendy and me making up the third side, and his mother standing in the middle.

As soon as the colt noticed that we were heading his way, he scooted around the front of the mare. He stood with his nose toward the corner of the fence and his butt toward Wendy. She made her way ever so slowly up to the mare's hip and, as gently as she could, reached out and touched the colt near the head of his tail. That was enough to send him scurrying around the front of his mom where he found himself standing face to face with me.

It was pretty clear by the expression on his face that he wasn't expecting to see me standing there and, much to his dismay, he suddenly found his escape routes rather limited. Thinking as quickly as he could, he found the only open escape route possible and took it. Ducking his head, he turned and darted under his mother's belly, only to run smack-dab into Wendy. This caused him to panic a little, forcing him back the same way he'd just come. As he emerged on my side, he found that instead of completely blocking his escape route back out into the corral, I was standing as close to the mare's hip as I could, with an opening between the fence and myself. He no sooner saw the opening than he bolted for it, which was exactly what I was hoping he'd do. As he ran past me, I reached out and grabbed him around the neck with both arms, and away we went.

I wanted to get a good hold on him and get him under control just as quickly as I possibly could. Once I was able to do that, we could get a halter on him and hopefully get started on his training. However, I failed to take a couple of little things into consideration when I formed this plan. The first was his determination to keep me from getting him under control, and the second was the three or four inches of freshly fallen snow from a recent storm. Neither, I was to soon find out, was going to make my job any easier.

As soon as I got my arms around him, he took off running for all he was worth. I was only able to run alongside him for three or four steps before nearly losing my balance and falling face first into the snow. Luckily, before that happened, I'd decided that the best way to get him stopped was simply to lock my feet in place, lean back, and let him drag me. That was another slight miscalculation on my part. As it turned out, I had completely underestimated the little fellow's strength. That, coupled with my complete lack of footing in the snowy corral, sent me for more of a ride than I'd originally bargained for.

I could hear Wendy laughing from clear over on the other side of the corral as that little colt, running as hard as he could, dragged me first one way then the other. We made several complete laps around the very center of the corral before switching speeds and turning a very nice figure eight. Having finished our figure eight, we once again picked up speed and headed for the far end of the corral. It was about that time, I guess, that two things happened. The first was that I was finding it extremely hard to see because of the snow that was coming off the toes of my boots, flying up in the air, and hitting me in the face. The second was that the colt was finally starting to play out a little. Unfortunately, as I worked to reposition my feet to help stop the flow of snow in my face, the colt began to lose his balance and our legs became entangled. The result was predictable. We fell, tumbling several times end over end before finally coming to an abrupt halt at the far end of the corral. We both sat upright, covered in snow and out of breath, looking at each other for several seconds, before the colt started to scramble to his feet in another attempt to escape. As quickly as I could from the squatting position I was in, I reached up and tried to get another grip on the colt. That time, however, it appeared as though I was going to fall a little short.

My hands quickly slipped from around his mane, to his back, to his butt. I couldn't believe it. After all that, it suddenly looked as though I was going to lose him. I hated for that to happen for the simple reason that, without having a happy ending to the situation we'd created, the chances of getting close enough to the colt to catch him a second time were next to nothing, and I might have had to resort to roping him in order to catch him, something I really didn't want to do. I'd already started to feel sorry for myself, figuring he was gone, when suddenly I felt my left hand grab hold of something solid. I couldn't believe it. As luck would have it, I had gotten hold of the last possible thing—his tail.

He pulled me to my feet as he lunged forward, which was all the help I needed to get my right hand up and on his tail, too. With both hands gripped firmly around his tail, I once again locked my feet in place, and we were off, the colt running for all he was worth, and me skiing helplessly behind.

"Hang on," I heard Wendy laughingly say from her position over by the mare. "You've got him right where you want him this time."

We took off along the fence line, making a short turn to the left, which caused me to lose my footing for just a second. Having regained my balance, I noticed the colt beginning to slow down considerably. This time it was plain to see that his enthusiasm for escape was quickly diminishing, and we went only a few more yards before he slowed to a walk and grudgingly came to a stop. After all that, we'd finally accomplished what we set out to do in the first place—get the colt to stand still.

He was visibly tired, out of breath, and sweating, as I cautiously left my position near his butt and began to make my way along his left side and up to his shoulder. Once I reached his shoulder, still holding his tail with my right hand, I slid my left hand across his chest and up the right side of his neck. That gave me a pretty good hold on him, which was lucky for me, because I'd just gotten in that position when he began to struggle. He shook his head, reared, kicked, and tried to lunge forward, but it was to no avail. That time he wasn't able to break loose from my grip, nor was he able to get good enough footing to take me on another impromptu skiing trip. As a result, he not only quickly stopped struggling, but he also began to relax somewhat.

As is the case in most situations like this, once the colt realized that he wasn't being hurt or eaten and that neither running nor fight-

ing was getting him out of the predicament he was in, he was able
to allow himself to calm down. That was the first step in getting him
to start trusting people, and it would be what we did next that would
either allow us to build on that trust or ruin it.

At that point, if we had misunderstood him and interpreted his
behavior as being belligerent or mean and then reprimanded him for it,
we most certainly would have destroyed the trust he was beginning to
develop. No matter what we did after we reprimanded him, no matter
how nice we were to him or how kindly we treated him, he would have
always remembered that just at the critical time when he was beginning
to trust us, we let him down. He would have always thought of us as
an animal of inconsistent behavior and one that should be looked on
with suspicion. Training would probably have been very slow, because
the colt would have always been waiting for the other shoe to drop.
He'd be wondering when we'd hurt or scare him next because he'd
reacted or behaved in a way that was beyond his control. He'd always
be afraid to make a mistake when he was around us and, as a result,
he'd be less likely to respond to new things we tried to show him, for
fear he'd do the wrong thing and be punished for it. Put simply, without having the colt's trust, you never have the colt.

However, if at that point we showed the colt that we not only
understood why he acted the way he did but also helped him overcome his fear of us and the situation, we could start building on the
fragile trust that he'd begun to put in us.

With that in mind, Wendy came over, and while I still held the
colt, she very slowly and carefully slipped a small blue halter over his
nose and buckled it in place. She snapped a ten-foot cotton lead
rope onto the halter and, as she held the lead rope and I held and
directed the colt, we began to make our way back to the mare. Once
the colt realized where it was that we were going, he tried several
times to break loose and get back to his mother on his own.
Fortunately, I had a good grip on him and he wasn't able to get away.
This helped to reinforce the fact that it wasn't going to do him much
good to fight with us, while it was showing him that we weren't trying to hurt him and that together we were going to get him where he
wanted to be—by his mother. Hopefully, by getting him back to his

mother, he would begin to look upon us as allies instead of as ene-
mies, which would be the first step in forming the bond of trust we
needed if we were going to get anything done with him at all.

It took some doing, but after a time we were able to get him over
to the corner where his mother was tied and waiting patiently for us
to arrive. We let the two get reacquainted by smelling and nuzzling
each other before directing the colt back to his mother's udder, where
he immediately began nursing. We let him eat his fill and after about
five minutes, with his belly full, and exhaustion from his recent exuberant exercise overcoming him, he fell asleep while still on his feet.

He slept for about fifteen minutes and it was shortly after he awoke
that we started his training. Now, most people probably think that the
first thing this or any other colt should be taught is how to lead. That
wouldn't be a bad guess. Leading properly is one of the first and most
important things any young horse should learn. However, in this
colt's case, we thought it was more important to teach him how to be
caught. After all, his knowing how to lead wouldn't do us much good
if we couldn't get close enough to catch him. The problem that we
were up against was that he wasn't a very willing participant and if we
were simply to turn him loose and try to catch him again, we probably wouldn't have much luck. We needed to use a little different technique in helping him learn how to be caught.

We decided on a technique that I'd used in similar situations and
had always had pretty good results with. While holding on to the lead
rope, I let the colt wander wherever he wanted, providing he didn't
get any more than a couple feet away from me at any given time. If
he did or he tried to run off or pull away from me, I'd gently turn his
head in my direction and hold it in that position until he quit struggling. As soon as he stopped struggling, I'd give him some slack and
let him stand and relax for a few seconds. Then I'd slowly approach
him and gently pet him on his shoulder, neck, and face. If he started
to struggle while I was approaching him, I'd simply stand still and let
him fight against the lead rope. As soon as he quit fighting, I'd once
again give him some slack, let him relax, and start approaching again.

I repeated this over and over until he would stand quietly and no
longer tried to run off whenever I got near him. After about half an

hour he was standing and letting me approach and pet him from just about anywhere on his left side. His reward for doing that was returning to his mom, who was never very far away anyway, to nurse. After an hour of working with him, it was easy to see that he was not only starting to feel comfortable with Wendy and me, but he was also becoming a whole lot more receptive to what we were trying to show him. Typically that would have been a good place to quit for the morning. However, there was one more thing that we needed to show him before we could turn him loose.

From past experience, I knew that once we got the colt's halter off him, he probably wouldn't want us to put it back on. The reason being that even though he'd been wearing a halter the whole time we'd been working with him, we hadn't taught him how to accept one being put on his head. This is where a little understanding goes a long way. Many people don't realize that for a young, inexperienced horse, having someone put something on its head can be frightening and can even appear life threatening. Not only that, but the whiskers on a colt's muzzle and around its eyes are very sensitive and having something as abrasive as a halter rubbing against or across them will usually cause a colt to become pretty agitated. The colt will toss and shake its head and even try to get away from you when you begin to pull a halter over its nose. We needed to teach our colt how to accept a halter being put on and, in a sense, sort of desensitize him to the idea.

Before turning the colt loose, we brought an adult-sized halter out, and while I held him gently around his neck and also held on to the lead rope attached to the halter he was already wearing, Wendy slipped the large halter on and off his nose. As we expected, he fought pretty hard the first few times the halter brushed across his whiskers. However, after five or ten minutes of putting the oversized halter on and taking it off, he began to quiet down considerably. In fact, he became so accustomed to the feel of the thing being put on that after a while he began putting his head down and sticking his nose in the halter each time Wendy got it anywhere near him. Once he was doing that, we figured it was probably safe to turn him loose.

Before we did, I made sure that I'd be able to approach and halter him on my own. I did this by unsnapping the lead rope from the halter he was wearing and letting him walk away from me. As I expected, he went over to his mother and began nursing. When he was finished, I slowly made my way over to him, which he allowed me to do. I petted him on his shoulder for a few seconds before raising the adult-sized halter that I was carrying and placing it in front of his nose. I was happy to see him quietly drop his head and stick his nose right down in it. Apparently, we'd accomplished what we had set out to do. He not only understood that we weren't trying to hurt him, but he also understood how to be caught and haltered.

Over the next several days I continued to work on catching and haltering him, but we also progressed to some of the other things that he'd need to know. For instance, I began to show him how to lead properly from both sides. I did this by looping a long cotton rope around his butt and asking him to come forward by applying forward pressure on the lead rope attached to his halter. If he didn't respond or tried to protest, I'd put some pressure on the rope around his butt. As soon as he offered to move forward, I'd release the pressure on both ropes, rewarding him for a proper response. By working with him in this quiet and methodical way, he quickly learned that it was easier to follow me than it was to fight me. As a result, he was following me all over inside the corral within an hour after I first started to show him how to lead, and he was doing it without protest.

In fact, I soon found that as long as I worked with the colt in a way that he could understand, he usually picked things up quicker than any other colt I'd ever worked with. Within two weeks after Wendy and I first started working with him, he was not only easy to catch, halter, and lead, but he would also carry jackets and blankets on his back, allow his feet to be picked up and handled, and would load into a trailer on his own. Within a month, he would come when called, cross water and other obstacles, and allow himself to be saddled and cinched. Within two months, he would longe in both directions at a walk, trot, and lope, and would whoa, all on voice commands. Within three months, he would longe anywhere, anytime, without any kind of restraint, all on voice commands, including stopping and standing.

By the time he was two years old, we had done so much with him, showed him so many things, and gone so many places, that when it was time to get on his back for the first time, I was able to put a saddle and bridle on him, climb in the saddle, and go out on the trail for a short ride. He walked up and down the trail, crossing streams, stepping over logs, and letting me open gates from his back. Things like paper sacks blowing past him, rabbits scurrying to and fro, and horse-eating mail boxes didn't even faze him. He was as calm as a twenty-five-year-old gelding that had been everywhere and done everything. All this from a horse that had been given to me as a wild and spooky little baby that had wanted nothing at all to do with people.

Over the years I've had the opportunity to work with more colts than I care to remember. The one thing that seems true for them all is that when they are handled with some respect and understanding, they learn easier and faster. When they are handled with heavy hands and ignorance, they usually don't learn at all and often end up fighting their handlers every inch of the way. It's those colts, the ones that are forced to do things instead of being asked to do them or shown how to do them, that often end up causing the most problems for their owners as they get older. Many times it's the horses that were started with heavy hands that don't like to be caught. Sometimes they're the ones that won't allow themselves to be shod, bite at you when you walk past them, or kick at you when you walk behind them. Sometimes they're the ones that refuse to load into trailers, buck or rear for no reason, or suddenly act up in the show ring. They have a general lack of trust and respect for people and will show their disdain every chance they get, no matter where they are or who is on them.

I think what many people don't realize is that in order to have a good horse, you've got to start teaching it well as a baby. It seems to me that the key is knowing how to work with the colt in a way that is not only non-threatening to it but also is easy for it to accept. Just understanding how babies perceive the world around them is often the first step in being successful with a colt's training.

For instance, a baby will instinctively learn much of what it needs to know by watching older horses. The key word here is "watching." In other words, the older horses teach the younger ones by example, not by direction. This is a very important thing to remember when working with a baby. It's very seldom that a young baby is forcefully reprimanded by an older horse in a herd situation. If a baby does something wrong or in some way annoys or mistakenly threatens an older horse, the older horse will usually reprimand the baby with a threatening gesture or a dominant pose or posture, which lets the baby know it has done something wrong. Because of this, the baby learns how to trust and respect its elders, as well as learning right from wrong in the herd, often without physical punishment. Since that's the case, it only makes sense that a baby horse isn't mentally prepared to deal with being physically punished.

When we are working with a young baby, if we take it upon ourselves to strike, hit, kick, or otherwise physically intimidate the colt for something that we think it's doing wrong, then chances are we're setting ourselves up for a lifetime of disagreements with it. On the other hand, if we can teach the baby how to trust and respect us by finding ways to work with it, by showing it that the easiest way out of tough situations is by allowing us to show it the path of least resistance, then we will be on our way to developing a relationship that will be beneficial to both horse and handler. Of course, by saying this, I'm certainly not trying to imply that babies should never be reprimanded for improper behavior. After all, just as in the herd, they need to know what is acceptable and what isn't. What I am saying is that reprimanding unacceptable behavior doesn't always have to involve physical punishment.

I think the thing to remember here is that if you can help a baby develop a good mental attitude toward people when it's very young, chances are it will carry that attitude its entire life. By the same token, if a baby develops a bad attitude toward people, it will probably carry that attitude its entire life, too.

"I'll let you in on a little secret," I remember the old man telling me years ago. "Just because a colt is bred good or looks good doesn't guarantee he's going to be good. The only guarantee you have of that, is you and how you handle him." In my opinion, truer words were never spoken.

7

A Good Start

WHILE VISITING WITH a friend at the stable where he boarded his horse, I happened to notice a fellow doing some ground work in the nearby round pen. The horse he was working seemed very familiar to me so I moved closer to get a better look. Sure enough, it turned out that I did know the horse. He was a big bay gelding named Jasper that I'd ridden some years ago while helping a neighbor move some cattle. He was a very well-trained ranch horse that, by generous estimate, was on the back side of twenty years old. Because he was starting to get a little age on him, a couple of years back my neighbor had decided to sell him and replace him with a younger horse. I had always wondered where old Jasper ended up and, frankly, was surprised to see him there.

Jasper's new owner, a younger fellow who seemed a little brash and full of himself, was standing next to him in the round pen and appeared to be putting on somewhat of an impromptu training demonstration. As I approached, I could hear him explaining to a couple of onlookers some of the control techniques he was about to perform on the old gelding.

"To get the horse to move over," he said, "you swing your lead rope right here until he yields to the pressure."

He began to swing his lead rope, a long nylon thing with two leather strips braided in the end, at Jasper's left shoulder. Unfortunately for the man doing the demonstration, Jasper had long ago become accustomed to the sight and sound of ropes swinging around him. As a result, the whirring sound of the lead rope didn't mean anything to Jasper and he stood contentedly as if being fanned by the thing. After several minutes it was obvious that the man was becoming agitated at Jasper's indifference to the rope. In an effort to get a reaction, any reaction, he popped Jasper on the shoulder with the end of it. Startled, Jasper jumped backwards.

"No," the fellow shouted, "not back!" He slapped the lead rope on Jasper's butt, sending him lunging forward, almost into the man's front pocket.

"Dang you!" he yelled, banging away on the lead shank as Jasper, head high, pedaled backwards.

Thirty minutes later, after a seemingly endless barrage of popping, banging, hitting, and cussing, both horse and man stood in the middle of the round pen sweating and out of breath.

"What I have done," the fellow gasped, as he stood bent over with his hands on his knees and beads of sweat dripping off the end of his nose, "is show this horse that I'm the boss. Now that he respects me as being his superior," he puffed, "he'll do whatever I tell him to do."

Then, to prove his point, he took Jasper into the adjacent riding arena and jumped on him bareback with nothing on the horse's head but the halter and nothing to steer him with but the lead rope.

"When you have the horse's respect and total control of his mind," the fellow explained, still a bit out of breath, "you don't need a bridle or saddle to ride him."

I could feel myself wince as the man grabbed a handful of mane and hooked Jasper with his spurs. Jasper stampeded for the other end of the arena as if he'd been shot out of a gun. A typical reaction, I guess, for a horse that has chased cattle all his life and understood what the business end of spurs was all about. The man, looking as though his demonstration wasn't working out quite the way he'd originally anticipated, decided it was time to bring it to the most graceful ending he could. With that, he pulled up on the lead rope with all his might, in a desperate attempt to get the big gelding to whoa. Unfortunately, while pulling on the rope with both hands, he was also unconsciously clamping on with his legs and digging into Jasper's sides with his spurs. That, of course, was Jasper's cue to speed up, which he seemed to do with all the enthusiasm he could muster.

It was one of those situations that you run into every once in a while, where you just know there's going to be a wreck. It was inevitable. The only question was how bad it was going to be. As it turned out, I didn't have to wait very long to find out, because the whole thing came to a head at the far end of the arena when Jasper turned north and his rider unceremoniously went south.

Still holding the lead rope, the man flipped off Jasper's back, landing in a kneeling position. This forced the weight of his body downward, pushing his backside squarely down onto the rowels of his spurs, which somehow caused one of the spurs to become hooked in the back pocket of his jeans. No sooner had this happened than the slack was pulled from the lead rope, jerking the fellow right off the ground. He bounced real good a couple of times before letting go of the rope. He landed on his face and slid about five feet before finally coming to a stop. Jasper went only a few more feet before the loose end of the lead rope hit the ground. As soon as Jasper felt the lead rope on the ground, he slammed on the brakes and stopped dead in his tracks—the result of the ground-tying lesson he'd learned years earlier, about the same time his new owner was learning how to tie his shoes for the first time.

"You may want to let the horse be the boss for a while," I heard somebody yell. "If he respects you any more, he's liable to kill ya."

As the fellow dug himself out of the hole that he'd plowed with his head and then squirmed around attempting to get his spur out of his pocket, I couldn't help but think how much easier he could have made his situation had he only understood what it was he was doing. More and more people, it seems, try to go about training and work-ing with horses like this fellow did, with the touch and feel of a lumberjack. It seems like they look at it as if it were a competition, a survival of the fittest, if you will. They seem to want to prove their superiority over the horse, instead of trying to develop a partnership with it. It never seems to fail, either, that the ones who are trying so hard to prove their superiority are also the ones who end up face first in the dirt. It's too bad, too, because it's those people, the ones who look at a horse as something to overpower and dominate, who will never know just how good a horse they really have or might have had.

Personally, I just can't help but count myself as being very lucky each time I see someone like the fellow who was trying to work with Jasper. At a very early age I was shown how to work with horses by someone who truly cared about them. The old man was a person who didn't just work with horses, he lived horses. He looked at training as a form of communication that meant the difference between having a horse that anybody could use at any given time and a horse that a few people could use every once in a while.

I recall one gelding in particular that the old man worked with, where his skill, patience, and understanding transformed him from a horse destined for the killer pen to one that was able to prove himself time and time again, not only as a working ranch horse, but also as a roping horse, a barrel horse, and finally as a 4-H prospect for a ten-year-old girl. The old man bought the horse, a five-year-old sorrel gelding, from a lady who had kept him in her backyard since he was born. The horse had been treated more like a household pet than the sixteen-hand horse that he was. He was halter broke, but just barely, and when the woman came down with a terminal illness, she suddenly found herself forced to sell him. With sadness, she ran an ad in the local paper, and several prospective buyers had shown up to have a look at him. Unfortunately, the only people who were at all interested in him were the killer buyers. Nobody else wanted him for the simple reason that he was big, untrained, and appeared very spoiled. Nobody, that is, until the old man went to have a look at him. The old man apparently saw something in the horse that no one else had and, as a result, he worked out a deal with the woman and bought him.

Frankly, I didn't have very high hopes for the big gelding and I remember thinking that the old man had perhaps made a mistake in buying him. The gelding's name was Bennie, and all he did for the first week and a half after he arrived was pace the inside of his pen. Whenever anyone came close to him, he'd head to the far end of his pen, turn his butt to the person approaching, and shake uncontrollably. He refused to eat much and had lost quite a bit of weight in that short time. He was difficult to catch, he didn't lead very well, and everything seemed to scare him.

I happened to mention to the old man, about two weeks after the horse had arrived, that he didn't seem to be getting any better and that I sort of wondered if maybe selling him might be the thing to do. The old man just smiled.

"I'm sure we'll sell him," he replied, "but not just yet."

A couple of weeks later, on a day when the dust was being blown around by an unusually warm, strong wind, I noticed the old man heading toward Bennie's pen with a halter in his hand. Having just finished my chores, I followed him over and watched intently as he entered the pen. The gelding immediately headed for the opposite end of the pen, turned his butt to the old man, and started to shake. The old man stood at the gate and, with the halter in the crook of his arm, took out a cigarette and lit it, having to cup his lighter in his hand and make several attempts before finally getting it lit. Once he had taken the first long drag from his cigarette, he slowly and deliberately began to make his way toward the gelding. The horse responded to his presence by spinning on his heels and taking off at a dead run along the fence. The old man made his way to the center of the pen and stood in one spot facing Bennie as the gelding ran frantically around him. For at least five minutes, Bennie continued to run just as fast as he could go before the old man slowly made his way to the fence, cutting him off and sending him running in the other direction.

The old man made his way back to the middle of the pen, where he contentedly stood, finishing his cigarette. After another five or ten

minutes, it was clear that the gelding was becoming pretty tired, and he soon slowed his pace. As soon as he did, the old man took a couple of slow, but obvious, steps backward. The gelding ran one more lap around the inside of the pen, then came to a stop. Again, the old man took a couple of steps backwards, which was enough to get the horse to throw a glance in his direction. The old man stood in the pen for a few more seconds, then turned and walked out. Just like that, Bennie's first training lesson was over. It was a simple lesson and one that was as basic as it could be. All the old man was saying to him was, I'm not here to hurt you. I didn't know it then, but without the horse understanding that one simple thing, nothing else would ever be accomplished with him.

The old man was very patient and diligent in trying to get that point across to the horse. As a matter of fact, he repeated the same thing over and over again every day for the next couple of weeks. He would enter the pen, walk to the middle, and stand quietly until the horse quit running. The old man refused to miss a day of working with the big, scared gelding. He did it rain or shine, windy or calm, hot or cold. At the end of those two weeks, it actually looked like he was beginning to get through to the horse. He could walk in the gelding's pen, go to the middle, and stand with the halter hanging on his shoulder or from his hand. Bennie, while still a bit nervous, no longer ran off and, in fact, would often times face him as soon as he went in. He still wouldn't allow himself to be approached by the old man, which, as it turned out, was the next item on the long list of things that he was going to learn.

I had been watching the old man work with Bennie every day since the beginning and had seen very little variation in what was being done. That is, until about two-and-a-half weeks had passed. On that day the session started just like every other session had, with the old man going in the gate, lighting a cigarette, then walking to the middle of the pen. This time, however, something was different.

The old man began by standing in the middle of the pen with the horse facing him but nearly twenty feet away. Then the old man slowly started to walk toward him. He'd taken only a couple of slow and very calculated steps before Bennie started looking scared and nervous. He turned his head away from the old man and, with his eyes wide open, appeared to be plotting his escape. I was as sure as I could be that he was going to run off, but much to my surprise, he didn't. This, I'm sure, was due to the fact that as soon as the old man saw Bennie's concern, he stopped dead in his tracks and allowed the gelding to get used to his presence at the new, closer distance. It took a few minutes, but Bennie did appear to relax some with the old man standing a little closer. As soon as he relaxed, the old man took a step backward, first to reinforce the fact that he wasn't in any hurry to get close to him and second to thank him for relaxing.

This went on for quite some time—the old man stepping toward the gelding, letting him relax, then stepping back—before any real progress appeared to be made. In fact, I would wager that nearly an hour had passed, with the old man inching his way toward the gelding, before he was finally within reach of the horse's shoulder. Once he was, he simply backed away without touching the gelding, then turned and left the pen. The old man repeated this step in Bennie's training for at least a week before attempting to touch him. However, when he did finally try, Bennie stood very quietly and allowed himself to be touched and lightly petted without even a hint of the terror that he'd shown when his training first began all those weeks earlier.

One thing that helped the situation was that the old man was wise enough not to make one of the most common mistakes people make when they're finally able to approach a horse that has previously been impossible to get near. People tend to immediately smother the horse with affection, that is, they pet and stroke it and may even try to hug the horse around the neck. While the person is simply trying to show the horse that they're happy to be next to it, the horse often mistakes this outpouring of affection as aggression. Of course, that causes the horse to panic and run off, forcing the person to start the process all over again.

The old man's way of touching Bennie for the first time was far from being smothering. While standing at the gelding's side, he slowly reached out and tentatively touched him on the shoulder. Once the horse had allowed himself to be touched, the old man just as slowly withdrew his hand. He did this a couple of times and then slowly backed away. He let Bennie stand quietly by himself for a couple of minutes before he approached again and repeated the whole thing. As the days passed, the old man was able to increase the area that Bennie allowed him to touch, until he could touch or pet him just about anywhere on his body. Another two weeks had passed before the old man could walk up to the horse, pet him on his face or body, and even walk around him without the horse becoming concerned. It was then, and only then, that he finally started teaching him how to accept being haltered.

Bennie had been halter broke at one time, so teaching him how to accept the halter was easier than it could have been. All the old man did was let him smell the halter a couple of times. Then he slowly slid it on and off Bennie's nose five or six times before finally buckling it in place. He even buckled and unbuckled it several times before attempting to lead him off. Surprisingly, ol' Bennie walked right off at the old man's very first request. I was surprised because, with the way Bennie had acted up to that point, it could have easily gone the other way. Frankly, I really doubted that he would lead. As it turned out, that would be just one of many times Bennie would prove my intuition wrong.

Over the next several months, the old man slowly eased me into helping with Bennie's training. Most of what I was doing was taking him out of his pen, leading him down to the main gate, around the front pasture, through the barn, and then back to his pen. At first, I just assumed that all I was doing was getting him out of his pen so he could get some exercise, but as time went on, I came to realize the importance of what we were doing. One of Bennie's biggest problems was that he had lived his entire life, until he came to the old man, in a thirty-foot by sixty-foot backyard. He'd never had the opportunity to get out and see the world. As a result, everything was totally foreign to him. He had no idea of what was okay to be around and what he should be afraid of. So, just to be on the safe side, he was afraid of everything. Gates scared him, buckets scared him, barn doors scared him, barns scared him. The old man had a few chickens around the place. They scared him. Telephone poles, rocks, gravel on the driveway, stacks of hay, cats, even the old man's truck scared him. (In Bennie's defense, the old man's truck scared *me* a little, too.) At any rate, I soon came to realize that what we were doing was getting him out, not so much to give him exercise but, rather, to let him get used to the world around him.

Getting out in the world, however, wasn't something that was high on Bennie's list of things to do, and for the first three weeks it was everything I could do just to get him out of his pen. Once I was able to get him out, I had to make sure that I stayed on my toes at all times because he spooked at everything, and I mean everything. I made the mistake, during one of our first trips away from his pen, of relaxing while we walked past the round pen. As we were making our way past it, a slight breeze came up, moving the gate slightly and causing its hinge to let out an almost inaudible squeak. Bennie not only heard it but also didn't it like very much. He was between me and the round pen, and upon hearing the potentially life-threatening squeak, he immediately jumped skyward, just far enough in my direction that he was able to land squarely on the little toe of my right foot. Now, there are two things that can happen when a 1,200-pound horse lands on a four-ounce toe. The first is that the horse may realize the error of his ways and apologetically lift his foot. The other is that the grunt of surprise and agony that one lets out as the toe breaks in two or three places may make the horse more frightened, causing him to mash down even harder. As I recall, it was the latter that occurred in this case.

At any rate, it took what seemed like a long time for Bennie to become comfortable enough with our daily outings that he was no longer spooking at noises, shadows, and objects. In fact, if I remember correctly, it wasn't until the following spring, nearly seven months later, that the old man resumed working with him on a regular basis. He told me the reason he waited so long to resume working with him was that he wanted to make sure Bennie could pay attention to what was being shown to him. Until Bennie was comfortable with his surroundings, he'd be spending so much of his time worrying that something was going to get him that anything we tried to show him would have to be repeated over and over again.

"If he can't pay attention," the old man told me, "he isn't going to learn. If we know he isn't ready to learn, why bother trying to teach him? In my opinion, it's more to our advantage to spend our time getting him ready to learn than it is for us to try to force him to learn."

It was an idea that made perfect sense to me. By spending extra time showing Bennie the world around him, we probably did make his actual training a whole lot easier for him and us. Of course, that doesn't mean that things didn't still frighten him, because they did. The saddle and saddle blanket, for instance, were two things that we soon found he didn't care for in the least. However, instead of making the mistake of trying to force them on him, the old man simply allowed Bennie all the time he needed to get used to them himself.

The way the old man did this was simple. He took the saddle blanket and tacked it to the top rail of Bennie's pen, just above his water tank. He also tied some baling twine around the horn of an old, worn out saddle and tied the string to the top rail of the pen, hanging the saddle just above Bennie's feeder. That way, even though Bennie was obviously afraid of the saddle and blanket, he was going to have to get used to them if he was going to get anything to eat or drink. The good thing about it was that he could get used to them in his own time. Surprisingly enough, his hunger and thirst must have been stronger than his fear, because in less than a couple of hours he had not only approached both items but he was also eating and drinking with them hanging over his head.

Even though Bennie appeared to have become accustomed to the saddle and blanket in a relatively short period of time, the old man left both of them hanging on the fence for over a week before finally taking them down. He did this not only to let Bennie get used to seeing them while they hung on the fence, but also so he could get used to them when they moved around, which they did any time the wind came up.

"It's the lazy man's way of saddle breaking," the old man told me. "What we're doing is just letting him get the tough part out of the way by himself—the part where he learns that the saddle isn't going to eat him. Once he understands that, the putting-it-on-his-back part should go a little easier."

It would be nearly a week and a half before I found out for myself whether the old man's theory of the horse "teaching himself" was going to work. As I arrived for work one morning, I noticed Bennie already standing in the round pen. Sitting on the ground in the middle of the pen were the old saddle and blanket that had been hanging on the fence of his corral. Bennie appeared to be paying no attention to them and, in fact, seemed to be dozing. As I went about my business that morning, I would head out to the round pen from time to time and check on him. I was surprised to see on one of my visits that Bennie had made his way over to the saddle and blanket and appeared to be investigating them. He was nudging them with his nose and pawing at them with his front feet. At one point he even picked up the blanket in his teeth and took off running around the pen with it. He'd made about two laps with the thing dangling from his mouth when he playfully flipped it backwards over his head. The blanket, having gotten quite a bit of altitude, floated over his back and was caught by a slight gust of wind. The gust caused the blanket to open up, changing its course in midair. It drifted slowly downward, landing neatly on the top rail of the round pen, as if someone had carefully placed it there.

Bennie spun around just as the blanket was landing and, having seen the precision with which he'd placed it on the fence, shook his head, squealed, and took off running and jumping, as if to say that putting the blanket on the fence had been his goal all along.

Unbeknownst to me, the old man had also made his way out to check on Bennie and was now standing quietly by my side.

"Who would'a thought?" he said, nudging me with his elbow. "A horse with a sense of humor."

The old man explained that by picking the blanket up and playing with it, Bennie was telling us that he was ready for the next step in his training—being under saddle.

"If he's comfortable enough with it to carry it," he smiled, "he's probably comfortable enough with it to wear it."

With that, he walked over, went inside the pen, and pulled the blanket off the fence. He shook it out, getting rid of the accumulated dirt, and then walked to the middle of the pen. By this time, Bennie had stopped running and was standing near the gate, facing the old man. Holding the blanket in both hands, the old man stood for a few minutes and then slowly made his way toward the horse. He stopped periodically during his approach, allowing Bennie to get used to the idea of someone walking at him while holding a blanket and letting him build some confidence in the situation. Surprisingly enough, the old man was able to get within arm's length of him in a very short period of time.

Once he was next to Bennie, the old man stroked him on the shoulder several times before slowly bringing the blanket around and showing it to him. Bennie acted a little surprised at the sight of the blanket but didn't try to move away or run off. Once Bennie had gotten a good look at the blanket and had spent some time smelling it, the old man lowered it to his side, stroked the gelding on the neck, and backed off a few feet. He repeated this several times, making sure that Bennie was completely comfortable with the blanket, before positioning himself at Bennie's side and slowly touching him with it. He touched him several times in the shoulder area before cautiously working his way up to his side, hip, neck, and finally rubbing it on his back. He went over to Bennie's other side and repeated the whole process before finally placing the blanket up on his back. He'd put the blanket on his back from both sides and had worked with him in such a way that Bennie had become almost oblivious to it. By the time he quit working with the blanket nearly an hour later, the old man could literally throw it on Bennie's back from six feet away, drop it on the ground next to him, and throw it under him and through his legs without the slightest sign of concern from Bennie.

The old man walked back to the middle of the pen, put the blanket down, picked up the old saddle, and slowly returned to the horse. Bennie showed very little concern as the old man approached with the saddle and, in fact, seemed almost happy that they were finally going to get down to the meat and potatoes of the session. The old man did many of the same things to get Bennie accustomed to the saddle that he'd done with the blanket, including showing it to him and letting him smell it, touching and rubbing it on both sides, and finally placing it gently on his back. Like the blanket, he worked with the saddle for nearly an hour and by the end, Bennie was completely comfortable with the sight, smell, and feel of it. At that point, the old man quit for the day.

The next morning the old man started all over again, beginning with the blanket and working his way up to the saddle. Bennie showed absolutely no sign of concern with either and, as a result, the old man progressed to the next step—getting him used to the feel of the cinch. He did this by placing a lead rope over Bennie's back and under his girth area. He then slid one end of the rope through the snap on the other end, creating a loop around Bennie's midsection. He slowly pulled the rope tight. Bennie didn't really care much for the feel of the pressure around his middle and tried to walk off a couple of times.

"The reason I use a lead rope for this instead of just cinching the saddle down on him," the old man explained, after Bennie was finally standing still, "is because if he doesn't like the feel of the pressure around him and he decides to blow, he isn't going to hurt this lead rope. If he blows with a saddle on, or half on, which is what normally happens, he'd probably not only hurt the saddle, but he'd likely hurt himself, me, and the round pen all at the same time." He paused, loosening the lead rope, then slowly tightening it again. "I'll just about guarantee," he continued, "when that happens, getting the saddle back on him a second time is not an easy thing to do."

The old man worked with the lead rope for nearly half an hour before putting it down and finally bringing the saddle and blanket over. Bennie stood perfectly still as the old man swung first the blanket, then the saddle, up on his back. He walked around to Bennie's off side and lowered the cinch, which had been secured to the saddle horn. Then he went quietly back to the near side and, holding the saddle's latigo in his left hand, reached under Bennie and got hold of the cinch. He brought the cinch up and gently pulled it snug a couple of times before passing the latigo through the cinch ring and slowly tightening it down for real. He allowed Bennie to stand with the saddle on his back for several minutes, during which time Bennie couldn't help but turn and sniff, nudge, and even bite at the leather fenders and stirrups of the saddle. After a while, the old man asked Bennie to move off by clucking and slapping his hand to his leg. Bennie obliged by taking four or five very tentative steps, stopping to have another look at the saddle, then breaking into a trot, and then loping at the old man's request. At no time did Bennie seem frightened or put out by having to wear the saddle, which, as the old man pointed out, was a very good sign in terms of his future training.

"If he'd went to bucking or carrying on after we put that saddle on him," the old man said, as Bennie loped effortlessly around him, "chances are, he would have done it when we got on him for the first time, too. The fact that he didn't tells us that he's comfortable with it on his back, which should make a difference once we try to get on him."

I was under the impression that we were going to try to get on him that day. After all, he'd been doing really well up to that point. However, the old man had other plans. For the next four or five days, he continued to take Bennie into the round pen and saddle him in the same way, although as time went by he was able to skip some of the preliminary things, such as showing Bennie the saddle and blanket before putting them on him. After saddling Bennie up, instead of getting on him, the old man would bring out his long cotton driving lines, hook them to Bennie's halter, and start ground driving him. He explained that before we got on for the first time, he wanted Bennie to know everything he could about what was going to be asked of him. The old man wanted him to know that backward pressure on the reins meant stop. More pressure meant to back up. When he felt pressure on the left rein, it meant to turn left, and pressure from the right rein meant turn right.

"By teaching him these things before we get on him," the old man told me, "we run less of a risk of him becoming confused and trying to unload us the first time we ask him to stop or turn."

It made perfect sense to me. Later I was thankful that the old man was taking extra precautions and time to cover all the bases because, much to my surprise, I ended up being the first one to get on ol' Bennie.

The old man had been ground driving Bennie for about a week and had even allowed me to try (although I must admit I wasn't very good at it), when one day, out of the blue, he called me into the round pen.

"I think he's ready," he said matter-of-factly.

"For what?" I asked, petting the big gelding on the shoulder.

"He's ready for you to get on him."

"Me," I gasped. "Why me?"

"Why not?"

"I've . . . ah . . . I mean . . . I'm . . . ah . . ." I knew I was trying to say something, I just didn't know what. "He's . . . I mean . . . I've . . . I haven't . . . I've never done nothing like that before."

"Neither has he," the old man quipped. "This should work out real good." He grabbed me by the elbow and took me over near the stirrup. "Now, before you try to get mounted, there's a couple of things you need to do first."

Yeah, I thought to myself. I need to make out my will, say my prayers, and call my parents to say good-bye, little things like that.

"Before you try to get on a horse that has never been gotten on before," he said, "you first need to teach him how to stand up under the pressure of your weight."

He grabbed hold of the stirrup and pulled it with all his might. The horse nearly fell over sideways. The old man continued to pull, with Bennie stumbling to the side, until he finally tried to brace himself against the old man. As soon as he did, the old man released the pressure.

"This is one of the only times in a horse's life," the old man said, "when he is taught to brace against pressure, instead of give to it. If we don't teach him this now, for the rest of his life, he will never know how to stand still when somebody tries to get on him."

With that, he pulled on the stirrup once again, and again, he almost pulled Bennie over. He continued to pull on the stirrup until Bennie braced against the pressure with everything he had each time the old man pulled on him. Then the old man went to the other side and repeated the whole process until Bennie would stand against pressure on that side as well. He had me repeat the whole thing on both sides until Bennie would stand up for me, too.

"Now he's ready," the old man smiled.

I was under the impression that he was expecting me just to walk up, stick my foot in the stirrup, and swing into the saddle. I'd been present once when a fellow had gotten on a colt for the first time using that technique, and I wasn't looking forward to the same consequences he'd suffered. In that fellow's case, the horse took one or two steps, then panicked and went to bucking and carrying on in a way that made him look like he was breaking in half. The rider ended up on the ground, having performed what could only be described as a beautifully executed unscheduled dismount. He lay there in the dirt and manure, I recall very vividly, colorfully cussing the day of that horse's birth, as well as the horse's mother's birth, his father's birth, the birth of his brothers and sisters, and that of any other horse that happened to have the misfortune of looking like him.

With that image burning a hole in my brain, I slowly began to make my way toward the big gelding, feeling as if I were going to the Last Supper.

"Hold on," the old man said, stopping me just as I was reluctantly getting ready to put my foot in the stirrup. "Before actually getting on, you might want to take a little time to get him used to the idea first."

I wasn't sure what he meant by that, but I was more than willing to stop and listen while he explained.

"Go slow and do a little at a time," he said, as he switched places with me. He put his left hand on the saddle horn and slowly lifted his left leg as if he were going to put his foot in the stirrup. However, instead of putting his foot in the stirrup, he simply bumped Bennie lightly in the side with his knee. Then he returned his foot to the ground. "Before trying to get on," he began, slowly raising his leg and bumping Bennie again, "let's first get him used to the things that might bother him when we do."

He bumped Bennie several times lightly in the side, showing him what to expect from most people, who often unconsciously bump the animal with their knee as they're mounting. He explained that when you don't desensitize a young horse before you mount for the first time, the chances are he will become frightened or, at the very least, annoyed when he feels a knee bumping him. As a result, he could end up moving away from you each time you try to get on. Desensitizing him helps to ensure that it won't be a problem for him in the future.

As soon as the old man was confident that bumping Bennie with his knee wasn't bothering him, he went on to the next step. He put his foot in the stirrup, put a slight amount of weight on it, and then took his foot back out. He did this several times, adding a little more weight each time he put his foot in the stirrup, until he was finally able to lift himself off the ground. When he did lift himself, he did so in very small increments, no more than about an inch or so at a time. He continued to do that for a long time before he progressed to lifting himself a foot or more off the ground.

As time went on, he worked his way to standing in the stirrup and leaning the weight of his upper body across the seat of the saddle. While he did that, he also swung his right arm, dragging his hand across the top of Bennie's butt as he did, then lightly slapping the fender on the opposite side of the saddle. He did that to simulate the feel of someone dragging their foot across the horse's butt, as some folks do when they mount, and to simulate the sight and feel of a leg being swung over the horse's back. He explained that because of the way horses' eyes work, a colt will often become frightened by the sight of a leg suddenly appearing out of nowhere as the rider mounts for the first time.

It had taken nearly forty-five minutes, but the old man finally felt that Bennie was comfortable enough that it was time to move around to his other side. Once on the other side, he had me repeat everything that he'd done—bumping Bennie with my knee, putting weight in the stirrup a little at a time, and finally standing in the stirrup and swinging my arm across his back. I did all of these things very diligently, working with him for just over half an hour, when the old man proclaimed that Bennie was ready for me to try to climb on.

He had me walk around to Bennie's near side and briefly repeat all the steps. Then, while I stood in the stirrup and swung my arm over Bennie's back, the old man walked over to where I could see him, nodded, then told me simply, "Go ahead." Up to that point I'd been feeling quite relaxed, because I'd been keeping my mind off the ultimate goal by busying myself with all the tasks at hand. That changed, however, when the old man gave me the green light to mount up. He'd no sooner made the suggestion than my heart moved from my chest to my throat. My mouth went dry, my hands started to sweat, and my knees started to shake.

"He'll be all right," the old man said reassuringly. "Just take your time and go slow."

I swallowed hard, took a labored deep breath, then slowly began to ease my leg over. It seemed like it took forever to get it done, but before long, I found myself settling down in the saddle. Now Bennie was a pretty big horse, standing sixteen hands or better. As I glanced down at the old man for my next set of instructions,

I couldn't help but think what a long way to the ground it would be if Bennie decided to unload me.

"Don't worry about your stirrup," the old man said, noticing that I'd been tentatively fishing for it with my right foot ever since I sat down. "You aren't going to be needing it."

"What if he does something?" I heard myself ask in an unnaturally shaky, high-pitched voice, even for a twelve-year-old.

"He won't do anything," the old man replied reassuringly. "Besides, you're not going to be up there that long."

"I'm not?"

"No," he smiled, obviously detecting a bit of relief in my voice. "We don't want him to think you're going to be living up there, do we?"

"Living up here?"

The old man slowly made his way over to Bennie's head and began gently petting him on the bridge of his nose.

"Have you ever heard the old saying, 'What goes up, must come down'?" he asked, motioning for me to step down.

I nodded my head while happily lifting my right leg, cautiously bringing it back over to Bennie's left side, and putting it back on the ground.

"Well," he said, as I slid my left foot out of the stirrup and put it, too, on the ground, "horses haven't. A young horse that has never been ridden before doesn't know that once you get on his back, you're eventually going to get off." He paused for a minute, then motioned for me to climb back on.

"Just like everything else during his training, he needs to know exactly what we're doing and what's expected of him while we're doing it. We need to show him not only that we want to get on him, but once we're on, we're also going to get off. If we don't, he's bound to get to thinking that maybe we're never going to get off. And that's where we could start running into trouble."

He stopped talking just as I once again slid down into the saddle. He let me sit for a couple of seconds, then motioned for me to get back down before he continued talking.

"You see," he started, "if we stay on him without showing him that we're going to get off, he could start to become confused and nervous. He won't be able to understand that we're just going to be on his back temporarily. He won't know that eventually we'll be getting off of him, and as a result of not understanding that, he may take offense to the idea that we have chosen his back to set up camp on. In his confusion, he could decide on his own that we have been on him long enough and, in turn, do something that will get us off."

It was just another example of the old man's training philosophy at work—trying to understand the horse's perspective, no matter what the circumstances. It was also the reason, I'm sure, that we spent the next half-hour doing nothing more with Bennie than getting on and off, not only from one side, but from both sides. Once we were sure that he was comfortable with the idea of someone mounting and dismounting, we quit for the day.

We started up the next day right where we left off—getting on and off—before getting ready for the next part of his training, having him move with someone on his back. As the first step, the old man brought out an old snaffle bit and gently slid it into Bennie's mouth.

Bennie had never been asked to wear a bit before and it definitely showed. He immediately began playing with it as though he was trying to spit it out. The old man let him wear it for the better part of the day, explaining that the only way he would ever get used to having a bit in his mouth was simply to have one in his mouth. There was no other way that he knew of to help Bennie get used to the taste and feel of one. He also explained that until Bennie found the comfortable spot in his mouth to hold the bit, trying to work him with it would be useless. He said that trying to stop or turn him would probably result in Bennie shaking his head and fighting the pressure that was applied, rather than giving to it, because he would be more worried about the feel of the unfamiliar object moving around in his mouth than he would be about responding to the cue.

By the end of the day, Bennie appeared to be quite comfortable holding the bit. Having seen that, the old man decided that his training could progress. We could finally teach him how to move with someone on his back.

This next step went pretty slow because Bennie had a terrible time learning to move comfortably with weight on his back. The added weight seemed to throw his balance off to the point that it felt as though he was going to fall over any time he moved. Gaining his confidence and balance was a slow, tedious process that took nearly a month and a half of riding every day. Our patience and persistence did pay off, however.

A couple of months after he'd been ridden for the first time, he had progressed from walking in slow, small circles in the round pen to trotting large circles and figure eights in the big arena, as well as taking short trips out on the trail. About a month later, we were loping big, fast circles and slow, small circles, taking long trips out on the trail, crossing roads, streams, and bridges, rounding up horses and cattle, and throwing a rope off of him. He was also loading in a two-horse trailer essentially by himself. He was responsive almost to a fault, in that the slightest amount of pressure from your heels would get him to move forward or change speeds. A shift of your weight backwards and a touch from the reins would get him to stop, no matter how fast you were going. A shift of your weight to one side or the other would get him to turn in that direction, and laying the rein on the side of his neck while giving the proper leg cue resulted in a world-class stationary spin.

Bennie's transformation was so complete that he didn't even appear to be the same horse that stood in the pen shaking uncontrollably when he first arrived at the old man's place. The most surprising thing about the whole situation, for me anyway, was that the old man seemed to know all along that with a little time, patience, and understanding we were going to be able to help that horse overcome his fears and become a productive and useful animal. The thing I'm still not sure of to this day is whether the old man had seen something in Bennie right from the start that made him believe we'd be able to turn him around or if he simply knew that he would somehow be able to get through to Bennie by what he did and how he did it.

The one thing I do know is that although it took almost a year, by the time he was finished, Bennie was one of the finest trail and working horses you could hope for. In fact, when it finally came time to sell him nearly two years after the old man had acquired him, Bennie not only brought top dollar, but he also had at least ten people who wanted to buy him. In the end, Bennie was sold to a fellow who used him extensively on his ranch until Bennie was nearly twenty years old, at which time he was sold to a family who used him for three years as a barrel and roping horse. He finished out his days with a young girl who started using him for 4-H when she was ten years old and he was twenty-three.

The memory of Bennie always seems to pop into my head right when I need him most. He usually comes to visit when I find myself getting in a hurry or when I start feeling that perhaps the horse I'm working with should be progressing faster than it is. Bennie is a constant reminder to me that good horses don't always develop overnight. Sometimes they develop over weeks, months, or even years. It all depends on where the horse is mentally and physically and where our skill is as trainer and teacher. After all, a horse will definitely have trouble learning at any speed if we aren't teaching in a way he can understand.

Fortunately for me, Bennie came into my life at a time when a lot of other young trainers were learning how to get as much out of a horse as fast as they could, by any means necessary. He was proof positive, at least to me, that the end result and the future quality of life for the horse are more important than the speed at which you arrive there. One thing the old man always used to tell me that I've found to be true on more that one occasion is that when it comes to training horses, the faster you try to go, the behinder you get. Put simply, faster is not always better.

From working with the old man and Bennie, I learned two very important things about working with horses that have turned out, even to this day, to be the keys to success. One is that a horse will only learn what we have to show him if we are showing him in a way he can understand. That, I have come to realize, is really the single most important part of working with horses. The other thing is that horses will almost always learn what we have to show them. We just need to remember that they can only learn as fast as they can learn, not necessarily as fast as we can teach.

8

The Lesson

I HAD JUST finished dumping the final wheelbarrow full of manure from the last of the six pens that I'd cleaned that morning, when I happened to notice the old man standing in front of the barn putting a saddle on one of his favorite horses, a sorrel gelding named Red.

"Have you got those pens cleaned?" he asked, as I leaned the wheelbarrow in its usual place against the side of the barn.

"Just finished," I replied, wiping the sweat from my forehead with the back of my hand.

For the past month and a half, we'd been experiencing what a lot of people were referring to as a drought. Not only had we not had any rain to speak of, but it had been hot, real hot. That day was no exception. By six o'clock that morning, the temperature had already reached seventy-eight degrees. By eight o'clock, when I arrived at work, it was eighty-five degrees. At ten thirty, as we spoke, the temperature was pushing ninety-five.

"Why don't you saddle up that new horse," the old man said, matter-of-factly. "Let's go for a ride."

"Isn't it a little warm for riding?" I questioned.

"It is now," he nodded, looking off to the west where a small cloud bank was beginning to form. "But it won't be in a little while."

I wasn't sure if he knew something about the weather that I didn't or if it was just wishful thinking on his part. At any rate, I did what he said. I made my way over to the pen where the new horse, a small, gray gelding the old man had bought at a sale about a week earlier, was standing. I haltered him and led him to the barn where I tied him next to Red, brushed the dust off him, and saddled him up. As I understood it, the gelding was ten or eleven years old and was supposed to be well trained, having been shown in both western and English pleasure classes for seven or eight years. From what I'd seen of him, he sure appeared quiet and willing to do whatever was asked of him. Only two days earlier, I had watched the old man riding the gelding in the arena out back. Even in the heat of the day, he performed everything asked of him without the least bit of fight or hesitation. I'd been hoping I would get a chance to ride the little gray before the old man sold him, and as luck would have it, it looked like today was the day.

I had just finished tightening the cinch when the old man came walking out of the tack room carrying two rolled-up slickers.

"Here," he said, setting one of the slickers on the back of my saddle. "You better tie this on. We might need them today."

No sooner had he spoken than a hint of a breeze came up from the west. I wasn't sure if it was because we hadn't had a breeze in a while or if what I was feeling was the real thing, but as soon as the breeze began to blow, it seemed as though the air cooled a little. The breeze also seemed to have a bit of an odor to it. It smelled like . . . rain.

Not really thinking much of it, we tied our slickers to our saddles, mounted up, and headed for the gate that opened out onto the trail. As always, the old man approached the gate first and, turning him parallel to the fence, gave Red a light cue with his heel to which he responded by effortlessly sidepassing to the gate. Red stood perfectly still while the old man, still in the saddle, bent down and unhooked the gate latch. Once the gate was unlatched, the old man sat back up and with another leg cue, turned Red on his front end so that he faced the gate. Red pushed the gate open with his nose and went through, with me and the new horse following close behind. Once through the gate, the old man brought Red to a stop next to it, grabbed the top of the gate in his right hand and gave him a light leg cue. Red stepped slowly sideways until the gate was once again closed, then stood perfectly still while the old man bent over and latched it. We could now be on our way.

There was enough room on the trail for the first quarter mile or so past the gate that we could ride comfortably side by side. However, as the trail narrowed and wound its way through a small wooded area, I gradually fell in behind the old man. We hadn't been out for more than about fifteen minutes when the old man laid his reins over Red's neck, reached in his shirt pocket, and took out his cigarettes. After taking one out of the pack and lighting it, he picked up his reins and began to relate a story that I had already heard several times before. It seemed as though it was a story he was reminded of each time he lit a cigarette while on horseback, and for some reason, he couldn't help himself from telling it whenever it popped into his head.

"I'll never forget the time," he started, "back in 1913, when I was cowboyin' for Oscar Buckner. I wasn't no more than about sixteen or seventeen years old, I guess, and had just taken up smoking a couple years before. Anyhow, there was me, Buster McCracken, Billy Whymer, and Sandy Sanderson. It was after calving season and we were heading out to start gathering the herd for branding."

I was behind the old man as we rode so I was unable to see the expression on his face. However, from the tone of his voice, it was obvious that this was a story that tickled him to no end.

"We were all on horses that were real green and pretty froggy, and before we left the wagon that morning we all put four bits in a can and drew names to see which one of us was going to get throwed first. Well, we'd been out a couple of hours when I decided I needed a cigarette. Those were the days when you bought your own makings and rolled your own, which was a dangerous proposition in itself considering how we were mounted that day. Anyhow, I'd gotten my cigarette rolled without too much trouble, took out one of my stick matches and, without giving it too much thought, lit the thing on the stitches of my saddle horn. That, as it turned out, was the mistake of the day. The sound of that match lighting was just the excuse my horse had been waiting for. He'd been wanting to blow up all morning and hearing that match flare was the thing that was going to get it done.

"No sooner had I busted that match head than he shied right into Buster's horse and then went to bucking. Well, Buster's horse reared up and somehow got one of his front legs over Sandy's horse's neck and his foot through the lariat that was tied to the saddle horn. That, of course, caused Sandy's horse to blow up and go to bucking, which pitched Sandy up onto Buster's horse's neck. Well, the whole mess rammed into Billy's horse and knocked him down, which only made matters worse. Both Buster's horse and Sandy's horse tripped over Billy and his horse and the whole works ended up in a pile on the ground. In the meantime, me and my horse went bucking across the prairie until he jammed me just right and sent me flying right off his back and smack into a prickly pear cactus." At that point, the old man couldn't help but stop and let out a heartfelt chuckle that lasted for the better part of a minute.

"Well," he continued, having regained his composure, "it was just our good luck, I guess, that none of us got hurt too bad and that the other boys were able to kick loose and get away from the pile they were in before any of 'em got killed. The bad part about the whole thing was that by the time the horses got themselves untangled and back on their feet, they'd pretty much decided that they didn't want to have anything else to do with us or going out and gathering cattle. So, before we could get any of them caught, they'd all turned tail and run back to the wagon just as fast as their legs could carry them. Now, it was bad enough that we had all been put afoot and had to walk all the way back to the wagon just so's we could gather our horses and get back to work. But even worse was the fact that none of us really knew who had hit the ground first during the wreck, and so nobody could collect the bet."

The old man could no longer restrain himself, and he suddenly burst into almost uncontrollable laughter that was very uncharacteristic of him. The sound of his laughter was always contagious, and even though I'd heard the story several times before and no longer found it as amusing as when I'd first heard it, I just couldn't help but laugh along with him. It wasn't until a couple of minutes later that his laughter started to subside, and as we exited the wooded area, he slowly shook his head.

"Those were the days," he said, almost under his breath.

He got very quiet, as if he were in deep thought, as we made our way down a gradual, sloped embankment, across a dry creek bed, and up the other rocky bank. He remained quiet for a couple of miles before pulling his horse to a stop, tipping his head back slightly, and sniffing the smells carried by the breeze that had come up.

"Better slicker up," he said, reaching around and untying the slicker from the back of his saddle. "It's going to be raining soon."

We had been heading east almost since the moment we had left the barn, and as far as I knew, the old man had never once looked back to check the cloud bank that had been forming in the west. In fact, it wasn't until he suggested putting our slickers on that I turned around to have a look for myself. What I saw as I looked behind us was a little unnerving. The small cloud bank that had been floating innocently across the sky only an hour before now reached from horizon to horizon, was black as pitch, and was gaining on us fast. Falling from the ominous-looking clouds was what appeared to be a wall of water.

"I don't like the looks of that," I said to the old man, as I hurriedly pulled the slicker from my saddle and put it on.

"It's a bad one, all right," he replied. "No thunder or lightning, though. Just a lot of rain. My guess is that it'll get us good and wet, then blow right past." He paused, studying the storm as it raced toward us. "I'll tell you what, though, why don't we head over to that old barn up ahead, just to be on the safe side."

With that, we took off in the fastest lope our horses could muster and headed straight for an old wooden hay barn that had long since seen better days. The barn was on the site of an old abandoned farm and was just barely standing. The closer we got to it, the clearer it became that the entire thing was leaning just a little bit to the east. Only one of its four walls was intact. The others were missing several boards and, in some places, whole sections. The roof, we found as soon as we went inside, wasn't much better. In fact, it not only had large, gaping holes just about everywhere we looked, but in the entire barn there was only one spot large enough to keep us all from getting soaked. We made our way over to that spot just as quickly as we could, and no sooner had we gotten there than the storm hit.

We'd been watching the storm approach through the open barn door, as well as through the openings in the walls, and I don't mind saying that what I saw wasn't very encouraging. The visibility between us and the wall of rain pouring out of the clouds was very good—we could clearly see every object between us and the storm. Houses, trees, bushes, and fences were all in plain view. That is, until the

storm caught up to them. As the storm passed over them, each object simply disappeared behind a gray wall of water. The noise the water made as it hit the ground was like none I'd ever heard before, and it, too, was a little unnerving. It sounded like thousands and thousands of stampeding horses, out of control and heading our way. In fact, the storm hit our impromptu shelter with such force that I don't think any of us—me, the old man, or the horses—were too sure whether it was going to hold together or not.

As the storm enveloped us, water poured through the old barn like someone had taken a giant bucket and dumped it on us. It took a few minutes, but we all finally felt confident enough that the barn wasn't going to fall down under the deluge, and that we could actually relax and just wait it out. We tied the horses to one of the barn's support uprights, dragged a couple of the old hay bales that were scattered throughout the barn to the one relatively dry spot, and took a seat. We both sat quietly for several minutes, watching the rain fall, when suddenly the old man began talking.

"You know something," he said, rather loudly, so he could be heard over the sound of the rain, "I've always kind of regretted having to use those horses that day."

"What horses?" I asked.

"The ones me and them other boys had that wreck with, back in '13," he replied, pulling his cigarettes out of his pocket and slowly shaking his head. "Those colts never were right after that."

He put a cigarette in his mouth and lit it, then returned his lighter to the watch pocket of his jeans before continuing.

"Those colts had no business being out chasing cattle that day," he said, as the smoke from the cigarette rolled out of his mouth and nose. "There wasn't a one in the bunch that had been ridden more than a time or two in their whole life. None of them had a clue as to what was expected of them." He paused, looking down at the ground, as though talking about the matter was an embarrassment to him.

"I'm sure they all would have made good horses, if we would have given them the chance. But instead, we made them do something they weren't ready to do and we ended up ruining 'em. We ruined every one of 'em."

This was a part of the story that I'd never heard before, and as he talked, I found it obvious that it was a part he wasn't very proud of.

"I was always brought up with the idea," he continued, having taken several drags off his cigarette, "that when you work with a horse, you should always leave him better off than when you started. If you can't do that, you have no business working with them in the first place. After I'd seen what we'd done to those colts," he slowly shook his head from side to side, "well, let's just say that I've never made that mistake again."

He flicked the growing ash from his cigarette into the palm of his hand, then rubbed his hand on his jeans, effectively getting rid of the ash without running the risk of starting a fire inside the old barn. As I watched him, I found what he was telling me a little hard to comprehend. After all, here was a man who had helped hundreds of horses just in the short time that I'd known him. For all I knew, he'd probably helped thousands more and maybe even tens of thousands more during his lifetime. Out of all the horses that had come and gone throughout his years, it was apparently the one he hadn't helped that had made the biggest impression on him.

"I learned a real important lesson that day," he said, mashing the butt of his cigarette on the heel of his boot, after taking the last deep drag. "That is that it's always easier to make a bad horse than it is to make a good one."

He got up from his seat on the old hay bale and walked over to Red. Another leak in the ceiling had developed and was dumping a steady stream of water right down on the seat of his saddle. The old man looked up to see exactly where the leak was coming from, then laid a gentle hand on Red's hip and moved him out from underneath it.

"Ending up with a good horse," he was still standing by Red's side and wiping the wet seat of his saddle with the sleeve of his slicker, "always takes some thought and a little understanding on the part of the person doing the training." He slowly threw a glance in my direction.

"Ending up with a bad one takes no thought at all."

Apparently, the old man must have felt with that, he'd made his point (although it would still be a little while before I'd understand what that was). He said nothing more about the matter. He simply came back over, took up his seat on the hay bale, and together, with him on his bale and me on mine, we looked out the door at the monsoon-like downpour of rain.

The water continued to pour down, outside and in, at that same rate for nearly forty-five minutes before starting to slow down. It took nearly an hour-and-a-half of waiting out the storm before it came to an abrupt halt, almost as suddenly as it had come on. It was then and only then that we slowly made our way out of the barn, free to be on our way.

We both took off our slickers, shook the water off them, and tied them back on our saddles before mounting up and starting back. As we got back on the trail, we quickly found that the ground was saturated with water, which made the footing in some places pretty slippery. There was also a good bit of standing water in the worn areas of the trail, and although I didn't give it much thought at the time, I did notice, as we approached each of the large puddles, that my horse was going out of his way to avoid stepping in them. I guess I didn't give it much thought because I didn't really see it as a problem or even a potential problem. I simply saw it as the horse not wanting to get his feet any wetter than they already were. It wasn't long, though, before I found out that simply wasn't the case.

We'd been easing our way, quite uneventfully, down the trail when we came upon the little dry creek bed that we'd crossed on our way out. The only difference was that it was no longer a dry creek bed. In fact, it was very full of rapidly running, brownish-colored water, eight feet wide and nearly eight inches deep. The old man eased Red down the gently sloped rocky bank and stopped him just short of the water.

"Did I happen to mention," he said with a slight grin, as he turned around in his saddle and looked up at me, "that the horse you're on has a little trouble crossing water?"

"No," I replied, a bit taken aback by this sudden revelation, "you didn't."

"Well," he said, once again facing forward, "he does."

He eased Red into the water, and without so much as a glance back in my direction, he and Red scrambled up the other bank and continued on their way, leaving me and the little gray horse to figure out on our own how we were going to get across. I could see a problem with this idea—I'd never worked with a horse that was water shy before and, as a result, didn't really know how to go about getting him to cross. I don't mind saying, either, that the thought of being left out on the trail alone in that situation wasn't very appealing to me. As the old man casually disappeared into the wooded area on the other side, my only thought was to get across that creek just as fast as I possibly could.

With that, I urged the gelding down the bank. He went with very little hesitation until he reached the very edge of the water. Once he got there, he simply locked up and refused to go any farther. Immediately, I began nudging him with my heels to try to persuade him to go on, but he would have none of it. In fact, he backed up a step or two. This, of course, wasn't the response I was looking for, and so to let him know that I wanted him to move forward instead of back, I quickly went from nudging him to kicking him. He responded to my kicks by turning to the left and trying to scramble back up the bank that we'd just come down. I grabbed the right rein and pulled his head back around so that he was again facing the water, only to have him go all the way to the right until he was heading up the bank in that direction. I pulled him back the other way, and he shook his head and jerked on the rein. I kicked him in the sides and he backed up. I slapped him with the ends of the reins and he tried to buck. I slapped him again and he tried to rear.

Twenty minutes later, I found myself out of breath and nearly played out. I stopped fighting with the gelding long enough to kind of regroup, only to find that after all that, we were standing on the top of the bank looking down at the creek. It was then, and only then, that the point of what the old man had been saying back in the barn while the storm raged hit home.

What he'd been trying to tell me, in a way that only he could, was that in situations like this, a little thought on my part would probably go a whole lot further than a lot of muscle. One quick look around was all I needed if I had any doubts about that. After all, for twenty minutes I'd been fighting that horse with everything I had, and we were farther away from our destination than when we'd started. It was pretty clear, at least to me, that my method of persuasion up to that point was definitely not the method that was going to bring success, and it was probably time to try something else.

First things first, however. Before finding a way to get the gelding to cross the creek, I first needed to back up and start looking at the situation from a little different perspective—his. I started thinking that if he hadn't been comfortable getting in the water before, I certainly hadn't helped boost his confidence by trying to force him to get in. It was now up to me to show him that, first, he could trust in me and what I was asking him to do and, second, that stepping in the water was nothing to be afraid of. The problem was that I'd just spent the better part of twenty minutes fighting with him for no apparent reason, and regaining his trust was something that was going to take a little doing and certainly some patience on my part.

I decided that the best way to let him know that I didn't want to fight with him anymore was to get off him and get him away from the area. By doing that, I hoped I could get him to settle down enough that we could start over. With that, I dismounted, turned him around, and led him away from the creek and back up the trail. After ten or fifteen minutes of heading away from the creek, I finally turned him around and we slowly headed back. Much to my surprise, he not only walked back toward the creek without much fuss, but he also allowed me to lead him back down the rocky bank to within about two feet of the water itself. It was there, two feet from the water, that he once again locked up and refused to go any farther. It was also there, two feet from the water, that I remounted. That time, however, instead of immediately demanding that he move forward, I simply sat quietly and allowed him to get used to the idea of being there with me on his back.

At first, it appeared as though he thought I was going to start fighting with him again, because no sooner had I mounted up than he became very tense and nervous. He quickly began moving his head from side to side as if looking for an escape route, he flicked his tail several times, and he even started to side step, first to the right, then to left. During that entire time, I tried to keep my legs off him and remain as quiet as possible, and other than keeping his head turned toward the water, I did absolutely nothing at all with my hands.

Very shortly, within ten minutes or less, he was standing quietly and no longer attempting to shy away. In fact, as he stood, he hesitantly dropped his head a couple of times, as if trying either to get a look at the water, smell it, or both. Taking this as a positive sign, I continued to let him stand and investigate for several more minutes before making my first attempt at getting him to move forward. When I did, I tried to make my cue as quiet and unobtrusive as possible. All I did was lightly cluck to him a couple of times, stop, then do it again. I kept on doing that until I got a reaction from him, and I didn't have to wait long. After just a short time, he again acted somewhat nervous, flicking his tail, moving from side to side, and lightly shaking his head. The difference was that after moving from side to side several times, he actually offered to move forward. As soon as I noticed his offer, which was really nothing more than a shift of his weight, I quit clucking to him and sat quietly for a few seconds, petting him on his neck and shoulder as though he'd just won the Triple Crown.

After letting him stand and relax for a few more minutes, I once again clucked to him, and once again received the same response, a nervous attempt at moving sideways before he finally made an effort to move forward. He then received the same response from me, as I sat quietly in the saddle, petting him lavishly on his neck and shoulder. Over the next half-hour or so we continued to inch our way forward in the same slow, tedious manner, until finally the toes of his front feet were almost touching the water. At that point I decided to give the situation a little more thought. The way I saw it, I now had one of two choices. I could either continue to urge him forward until he got in the water, or I could take this opportunity to give him, and me, a break and some time to relax.

Knowing for a fact that I was ready for a break, I just assumed he was, too. So, while he stood with his toes nearly in the water, I made the decision to back off for a while. I slid out of the saddle, petted him generously on his face, neck, and shoulder, then turned and led him back up to the top of the bank. We walked around for a good ten or fifteen minutes before making our way back down to the creek. This time he remained very calm and quiet and allowed me to lead him right up to the same spot where we'd quit, with his toes nearly touching the water. I climbed back on, and we picked up where we left off. After I mounted, I noticed a marked difference in the gelding. He was a whole lot quieter than he'd been when I was on him only a few minutes earlier, and he seemed more willing to respond to the cues I gave him. I had gotten on and clucked to him just once when he offered to move forward. Again, it was little more than a shift of his weight, but it was still a response and one that warranted a reward, which I gave him by once again sitting quietly in the saddle.

Much to my surprise, on my very next cue the gelding took one big step and placed his right front foot smack in the creek. He held it there for only a second or two before taking it back out, but at least he'd done it. Not wanting to rush him, although I had a nearly overwhelming urge to, I allowed him to rest and relax before giving him another cue. That time, he responded quickly by plopping his right foot into the water and holding it there while putting weight on it. I let him stand in that position for a few seconds before giving him another cue, to which he responded by stepping in with his other front foot. After putting both front feet in the water, he shifted his back feet forward as well, as if preparing to step all the way in. Before doing that, however, he suddenly began pawing at the water with his right front foot. He stopped, then started pawing with the other. Apparently that convinced him that what he was standing in was, indeed, water, and with that, he decided it was time to take a drink. He cautiously dropped his head, and I allowed him to drink his fill before asking him to raise it again and continue forward.

When I cued him, he took one tentative step forward with his right front foot, then his left rear, then his left front, then his right rear, and suddenly we were in the creek. Before I knew it, we were halfway across and the gelding had stopped and was pawing at the water with everything he had. In no time at all he had water flying in every different direction, and I kind of got the impression that he was getting ready to lie down. So, before he found himself getting too comfortable with that idea, I cued him forward once more. It seemed as though it took two or three good cues to get his attention, but once I did, he quit pawing and continued cautiously out the other side of the creek. It had taken nearly two hours from the time the old man first left us until we'd gotten out, but we had finally done it—we'd crossed the water.

As happy as I was that we'd finally gotten the job done, I just couldn't help but think as I sat on the top of that bank, staring down at the dirty water, that the old man had somehow set me up—he'd planned this entire day, right up to us getting caught in that storm and then forcing me to figure out how I was going to get that water-shy horse across a creek that he knew would be flooded when the storm was over.

At the time it was happening, I couldn't help feeling a little angry that the old man had taken it upon himself to leave me out there on my own, to "sink or swim" as it were. However, as time has passed, I've come to realize that he wasn't just playing an elaborate practical joke on me that day. Rather, he was doing what he did best. He was teaching. He was simply letting me see the difference between having him show me how to do something and figuring out how to do it on my own. He was letting me see that even though I'd never worked with a water-shy horse before, I could still overcome the problem by using patience and giving the situation some thought. Even more important, I think, was that he wanted me to understand the consequences that using force is bound to produce, and to always try to search for an alternative.

By doing what he did that day, he'd given me the benefit of his experience and tried to save me from making the same mistake that he felt he'd made with those colts all those years ago. He was trying to teach me the lesson he'd learned about training—that it's always easier to end up with a bad horse than it is a good one—and that there simply are no shortcuts when it comes to the latter. Most of all, I think he wanted to show me the one thing about training that he found the most important—we should always leave our horse better off after we've worked with it than when we started. By doing that, we're not only constantly improving our horse's behavior, but we're also improving our own skills, as well. After all, when it gets right down to it, isn't that our real goal anyway?

Tricks of the Trade

WE HAD BEEN waiting at the boarding stable for over thirty minutes before the fellow we'd come to see finally showed up. This particular fellow had called the old man the day before about a horse he had for sale. He said he was having a little trouble getting rid of the animal and would be willing to make the old man a pretty good deal if he thought he could use him.

As the fellow came over and introduced himself, I couldn't help but think that he didn't have the look of someone who would own horses. Not that horse owners look a certain way, mind you, it was just that this fellow seemed out of place. He was a small, thin man, wearing a white shirt and black pants, the kind of outfit my parents made me wear when we went to weddings or funerals. He also had on a pair of brown penny loafers, white socks, and thick, black-rimmed glasses. His hair was thinning on top and his skin was a kind of milky white— a stark contrast to the brown, leather-like skin of the old man.

Following the introductions, we made our way into the barn and up to the box stall where the fellow kept his horse. The horse was a black gelding that stood a little over fourteen hands tall and he was resting quietly with his head facing the back of the stall as we approached.

"What can you tell me about him?" the old man asked, as we peered into the stall.

"Well," the little fellow started, with just the hint of a Scottish brogue, "his name is Max and he's a pretty nice horse. He is easy to ride and he likes people. He's good on the trails and other related activities, and he is generally in a good mood, most of the time."

"I see," the old man nodded, smiling just a bit. "He's generally in a good mood."

"Oh, yes," the fellow replied, pushing his glasses back up on his nose with his index finger. "As a rule he is a very good sort of horse. He does have one irregularity in his behavior, however, which has forced me to reconsider his guardianship."

"He has an irregularity?" the old man asked.

"Yes," the fellow said. "And I don't mind telling you, it can be quite disconcerting at times."

"I see," the old man scratched his forehead. "What exactly is this irregularity, if you don't mind me asking?"

"Not at all," he smiled. "His problem, it appears, is that he develops a very violent demeanor whenever one attempts to put a bit in his mouth. He becomes quite contemptuous, really, and is often terribly frightening. I would be happy to demonstrate, if you'd like."

"Well," the old man smiled, "if it's not too much trouble."

"No trouble at all," the little fellow nodded, as he pushed his glasses back in place. "I'm happy to do so. I wouldn't want to misrepresent the animal in any way. I am simply not that type of person. In fact, I am quite confident that is the reason I have been unable to sell the horse. Whenever a prospective buyer witnesses his incredible behavior, they are immediately put off and negotiations cease."

"I understand," the old man smiled.

With that, the fellow went to the tack room and brought back a halter that he quietly put on the horse. He led the gelding out of the stall and tied him in the aisle, where he groomed him. When he'd finished grooming the horse, he went to the tack room and brought back his saddle and pad, which he carefully placed up on the animal's back and cinched down.

"You may want to step back a bit," the fellow smiled, as he took the bridle off the saddle horn where he'd placed it while tacking up. "He often becomes quite frenzied when I try to do this."

The old man stepped sideways a couple of paces and I ducked inside the stall as the little fellow began to lift the bit up to the horse's mouth. As he'd predicted, the horse threw his head violently skyward as soon as the bit touched his lips. Two more attempts at putting the bit in the gelding's mouth resulted in even more violent behavior. He not only threw and shook his head, but he also reared slightly and jumped up and down as well.

"That's okay," the old man said, as he slowly stepped between the horse and its owner. "I get the idea. Is he always this bad?"

"Sometimes he's worse," the little fellow said, his voice slightly raised. "A couple of times he has actually hit his head on the rafters of the barn." He adjusted his glasses, which had slid clear to the end of his nose.

"Did you know that this is a problem that can be fixed?" the old man asked.

"Yes, well, with all due respect," the man fidgeted, "you are not the first person to make that statement to me. In fact, I have allowed several knowledgeable horse people the opportunity to attempt to find a solution, only to find that the problem continues to worsen. If you feel that you can, indeed, alter Max's behavior, I will be happy to sell him to you, at which time you may work with him at your leisure."

"Fair enough," the old man smiled.

With that, the pair worked out a deal on the horse, and two days later the old man picked him up and brought him home. The old man didn't do a thing with the horse for about a week, but instead turned him out in the pasture. When he did finally take the gelding into the round pen to work with him, he did so in his normal, quiet manner, without fuss or fanfare. In fact, he'd probably been working with ol' Max for fifteen or twenty minutes before I even realized he had gotten started.

By the time I reached the round pen, Max was standing quietly with his head so low that his nose almost touched the ground. The old man was standing next to him, bent over at the waist, stroking him on his neck. He was holding a lead rope in his left hand that he slowly began rubbing the side of Max's head with. He also rubbed the horse's neck, face, and the top of his head with it before finally working his way down to the top of his nose. He spent quite a bit of time working the rope in that area before reaching down and lifting Max's head up. Once the horse's nose was at waist level, he very quietly and methodically began to work his thumb and index finger in and around the corners of Max's mouth. After about five minutes, and with very little protest from the horse, he was able to open its mouth by simply slid-ing his finger in the corner and applying slight downward pressure.

Once Max was willingly opening his mouth, the old man took the lead rope and once again rubbed the gelding's face and nose with it. Max showed very little anxiety, and before I knew it, the old man was holding the lead rope in the open palm of his left hand, as if it were a bit, and was pressing it softly to the horse's lips. He had the thumb of his same hand in the corner of the horse's mouth and was apply-ing a little downward pressure. He did this until Max quietly opened his mouth, at which time he simply slid the rope in, as if it were a bit. For the next half-hour, the old man continued to work with Max in the same manner, quietly sliding the rope in and out of his mouth. He must have felt confident that he'd accomplished what he'd set out to do, because after the thirty minutes or so of working with the gelding, he simply turned and left the round pen.

I was just a little confused about what he was trying to accomplish by putting that lead rope in Max's mouth. I mean, I knew he was try-ing to simulate the act of bitting the horse up—that was obvious. What I didn't understand was why he didn't switch over to the bit after he had the horse working so well. It seemed to me as though that would have been the natural course of action, but it appeared that the old man had no intention of taking it. So, as he was leaving the round pen, I asked him about it.

"Whenever I come across a problem like this," was his reply, as we headed toward the barn, "I always try to find a way of working with the horse that will be the easiest for him to understand and, at the same time, easy for him to perform." He pulled a fresh pack of cig-arettes out of his shirt pocket and whacked the top of the pack on the back of his left hand several times before opening it.

"My second priority, when working with a problem like this," he smiled, "is finding a way of doing it that's going to be the easiest on me. The last thing I want to do today is sit out here in the sun and wrestle with that horse."

"He looked like he was doing real well with the lead rope though," I said. "Don't you think he would've been all right if you'd switched to the bit?"

"What's the hurry?" he shrugged. "I don't want to ride him today. Besides, just because he'll take the lead rope doesn't necessarily mean he'll like the bit. You have to remember, the bit is cold and hard, and he's been hit in the mouth plenty of times with one. If I used a bit right now, he might just get to thinking that I want to hit him in the mouth, too. That could cause him to want to defend himself, which would probably turn the whole thing into a wrestling match." He paused. "See what I mean?"

"I think so," I replied.

"The way I look at it," he continued, lighting his cigarette, "I'd rather have him get used to the idea of me putting something in and out of his mouth without having to feel threatened by it. There's no way he would have allowed me to use a bit to do that, so I used something soft and non-threatening to simulate one—a lead rope."

He paused to look at the bottom of his boot, where a small horse apple had lodged itself in front of the heel. Leaning against the back tire of the tractor, he reached down and, with his thumb, popped the thing off his boot. He scuffed his foot on the ground a couple of times, making sure that all the residue was removed, before straightening up and continuing.

"He's just now getting used to the idea of me putting the lead rope in his mouth," he said, without having lost his train of thought. "If I all of a sudden switched over to the bit before he's sure I'm not going to hurt him, he may feel that I'm trying to trick him, and the trust he's built up in me would be gone. The lead rope is just a way of getting him used to me and the idea of taking a bit again, not a way for me to trick him into taking it. Understand?"

I did understand. It was just one more way of doing what he always did when he worked with horses. He was finding a way to get done what needed to be done while keeping the horse's perspective in mind. After all, why force the animal to do something it is obviously uncomfortable doing, when with a little thought and some ingenuity, the thing might be accomplished with a minimal amount of stress on everyone involved?

Over the years I've found that by keeping the horse's point of view in mind and by giving the particular problem some thought, a potentially stressful situation can often be overcome with little discomfort for both horse and handler.

I had one such experience quite a few years ago when I was called to look at a mare that the owner was thinking of selling because she'd had some trouble with her. It was midsummer and extremely hot on the plains where the horse was kept. As I pulled into the yard of the place, I could see a barn and corral in a small wooded area about one-hundred yards from the main house. In the corral stood a nice-looking palomino mare, frantically swishing her tail, shaking her head, and stomping her feet. As soon as I climbed out of my truck, a woman in her early thirties came out the front door of the house, walked up, and introduced herself as Nancy, the horse's owner. As we made our way over to the corral, she started to tell me about the mare's background.

She'd bought the horse two years before, in the fall of the year. At first, the mare was wonderful, going anywhere and doing anything that she was asked to do. The woman rode her sporadically throughout that winter and spring and never had even the slightest problem with her. It wasn't until the following summer that she began to have trouble.

"She doesn't like to be caught or handled," the woman said, as we approached the corral, "and she'll fidget like this all day and night without stopping. She doesn't do it in the winter—just when it's warm like this."

The cause of the horse's problem was painfully obvious to me, even without going into the pen with her to get a closer look. Just by standing at the rail of the fence, one could easily see that every fly, gnat, and mosquito in the county was trying to land on her. There were an awful lot of them getting it done, too, and they were doing a pretty good job of eating her alive.

"I'll bet that's your problem," I told her, pointing toward the swarm of insects on and around the mare. "They've got to be driving her crazy."

"I know," she replied, shaking her head. "I've tried to get some fly spray on her. I've tried to both spray it on her and wipe it on her with a rag, but it only seems to make her worse."

"It does?" I asked in surprise.

"If you think she's bad now," the woman said, "just try and get some of that spray on her. You'd think you were trying to hit her with a hot poker the way she carries on."

I wondered out loud if perhaps the reason the mare wouldn't allow herself to be sprayed or wiped down was simply because she'd never been taught how to stand still when someone tried. I suggested that it might be worth the effort to spend a little time with her and see if we could teach her to stand. The woman, unfortunately, would hear nothing of it. It turned out that, just that morning, she'd bought another horse and she had no intention of keeping or working with this one. Seeing that her mind was made up, I made her an offer on the horse, and a few days later we moved the horse up to the ranch where I worked.

It quickly became apparent why the woman had become so discouraged while trying to get fly spray on the horse. A couple of days after the mare arrived, I tied her to the hitch rail just outside the barn and brought out a plastic bottle filled with fly spray. Standing ten feet away from the mare and pointing the bottle away from her, I squeezed the trigger several times to work some of the spray into the nozzle. The sound of the air being forced from the nozzle seemed to take the mare completely by surprise, and she began to panic. She immediately shied away from the sound and pulled back with all her might. Instinctively, I guess, I stopped pulling on the trigger of the bottle. The mare, still a bit worried, stopped pulling back and stood snorting, with legs spread, eyes wide open, and nostrils flared.

I have to admit, I hadn't really been paying that much attention to the mare before I started to work the spray mechanism, and her reaction to its sound took me somewhat by surprise. I took a minute to let her regroup before I did anything else, and while she was calming down, I got to thinking about her reaction.

It seemed obvious that she had reacted to the sound out of fear, and the fact that she was tied to the rail, unable to get away, only seemed to make matters worse. It was clear that if I left her tied to the rail and tried to work with the spray bottle, the chances of one of us getting hurt during the process increased greatly. The biggest problem that I saw, however, was that without getting rid of the flies and gnats that were terrorizing her, the mare was virtually worthless.

She wouldn't allow herself to be handled, groomed, saddled, or ridden, and a horse with those deficiencies, I'm afraid, isn't much good to themselves or anyone else. For that reason alone, I felt it imperative to find a way to get her over her fear but, at the same time, to do it in a way that would put her through the least amount of stress.

After thinking over the situation, I decided that my best course of action was to try to desensitize her to the sound, feel, and smell of the spray. That meant that she was going to have to be very close to me as I sprayed the stuff around and on her. I needed her to become so accustomed to it that it just became part of life for her. Because tying her while I did that was too risky, I figured that it would be best to work with the mare in the round pen where she could run loose. By doing that, I hoped to keep her flight instinct intact as I sprayed the liquid in her direction. Hopefully, that would help limit her stress and give her the opportunity to see that I wasn't trying to hurt her.

Another problem I faced was that fly spray, at least the kind we were using at the time, was expensive. Trying to spray a horse moving at a high rate of speed in a round pen with a fifteen-dollar bottle of fly spray would prove to be very wasteful and extremely costly. As a result, instead of using a bottle full of the real stuff, I decided to fill an empty spray bottle with water and mix it with just a small amount of fly spray to give it the proper odor. Hopefully, by doing that, I'd be able to simulate effectively the feel, sound, and smell of the actual thing, at least enough to help the mare overcome her problem.

With that in mind, I took her down to the round pen and turned her loose. She slowly walked to the middle of the pen and stopped. I gave her a few pats on the neck to let her know that I wasn't there to hurt her, then backed up about ten feet. Standing on her left side, I pointed the water-filled bottle away from her and began working the spray mechanism. Her reaction to the sound was immediate. In a panic, she headed for the rail and took off running. It took about fifteen minutes and three refills of the bottle before she even thought about slowing down and stopping. As soon as I could see that she was offering to do so, however, I stopped working the sprayer in an attempt to reward her for a proper response. Each time she stood still, I'd go over and pet her, to help reinforce in her mind exactly what it was that I wanted her to do. Even with that, though, she would still take off running each time I began working the sprayer. That went on for the better part of an hour—me spraying water out of the bottle, and the mare running, stopping only for short periods of time.

It took nearly an hour and ten minutes before it appeared that she was finally trying to pay attention to what I wanted to show her. After that time, she stood, obviously still a bit nervous, and allowed me to spray the water around her and on her lower legs from a distance of about six or eight feet. At least the sound of the spray mechanism didn't seem to bother her nearly as much as it had when we first started. That was the major hurdle she needed to overcome, and once she did, things started to go better for both of us.

I continued to work with the mare in the same slow manner. About an hour and a half after we'd first entered the round pen, she was finally standing quietly and would allow me to move closer while spraying. Two hours after we started, she allowed me to spray with the bottle only inches away from her. At that point, I left the round pen and let her relax for about half an hour before returning. When I came back, I brought a full bottle of real fly spray along with the bottle of water. As soon as I entered the pen, I walked over and petted the mare to let her know, once again, that I wasn't there to hurt her. Then I backed up and, with the bottle of water, began spraying in her direction. She flinched and sort of offered to run off, but quickly settled back down and allowed me to approach. I worked with her until the water in the bottle was gone. Then I left the pen again for a few minutes.

When I returned, I took the bottle of real fly spray in with me and repeated the same procedure. She showed very little concern as I sprayed her from a distance of about six feet and, as a result, I was able to approach her with the fly spray rather quickly. She stood quietly and allowed me to spray her entire body, including wiping her face, with the very strong-smelling, undiluted spray. That, I figured, was enough for one day.

The following day I took her down to the round pen and we started the whole process over again. She settled down almost immediately, and within about five minutes, I was able to stand at her side and spray her entire body with the full-strength stuff. I worked with her in the round pen for two more days before I finally felt confident enough to try to spray her while she stood tied to the hitch rail. Much to my surprise, as I walked over and slowly began to spray her, she stood quietly, without any sign of the terror that she'd experienced at the rail only four days earlier.

The thing, I think, that really surprised me about the mare was that after we were able to get rid of the flies that were bothering her, she became a great horse. She was not only very kind and affectionate to everyone she came in contact with, but she was also one of the nicest riding horses on the place.

I could hardly believe that this fine horse had been given up on and sold by her previous owner for the simple reason that she couldn't get any fly spray on her. What surprised me even more was that the woman had apparently given up on the mare without really trying to find a way to overcome the problem. Oh, she had tried to spray the horse from time to time, but unfortunately, because of the way she did it, she actually made the problem worse. Tying the horse while she tried to spray her only served to enhance the problem because the horse would become frightened by the sound of the spray mechanism and start to pull back. Unable to get away from the sound, the horse's fright turned into panic, which scared the woman, who in turn stopped spraying. The horse learned that she could get the scary noise to stop by panicking and pulling back. Then, instead of trying to find a way to work through the problem that she inadvertently made worse, the woman simply gave up on the horse and sold her.

It was a perfect example of the kind of situation the old man had talked about. He'd said that when he worked on problems like this, he always found it to his advantage, and the horse's, to find a way of working with them that was easy on both him and the horse. Sometimes that meant working with horses in a way that was perhaps a little out of the ordinary. What he did was try to find a way to simulate the cause of the problem, as best he could, and then work with the horse in a way that caused the least amount of stress. In the mare's case, I found that simulating fly spray with water and allowing her to run loose in the round pen while I sprayed it toward her was the easiest way to overcome her problem with the least amount of stress on both of us.

There's another situation that comes to mind when I think about times I've used an alternative training method to overcome an annoying and potentially dangerous problem. It happened a few years back with a horse that I'd purchased at a sale. The horse was a big red gelding that was pretty well trained. Evidently, he'd spent most of his ten years on a cattle operation in Wyoming before he was sold to a cowboy who worked in a feedlot in northern Colorado. He was ridden for a couple of years in the feedlot before finally being taken to the sale barn where I bought him.

I brought the horse home and began riding him on the trails within a couple of days. I quickly found the gelding to be virtually bombproof—unafraid of everything, including cars and trucks that sped past him on the road, paper sacks that blew between his legs, and loud noises such as vehicles backfiring. I did find one noise, however, that he couldn't stand and that caused him to go completely ballistic whenever he heard it. That noise was the sound of electric clippers, the kind used to trim a horse's whiskers, fetlocks, and bridle path. You can imagine my surprise when I approached this horse with clippers for the first time, only to have him respond as though I was chasing him with a chain saw. He was tied to a small hitch rail near the barn door when I brought the clippers out, and his reaction to the sound they made was immediate. He panicked and pulled back, snorting and shaking his head wildly from side to side. He stopped only when I turned the clippers off.

At first, it was hard for me to believe that a horse that wasn't bothered by any of the things most horses are afraid of could be afraid of anything so insignificant as the buzzing of clippers. But he sure was. It terrified him. Just because I considered the noise insignificant didn't necessarily mean he felt the same way. And, when it came right down to it, it didn't matter what I thought. It was what he thought that was important.

I took the clippers back into the barn and put them away. I had to give the situation some thought because I wasn't sure that fixing the problem and getting him used to the noise of the clippers was all that important. After all, he was a great horse in every other respect, and if I really needed to clip a bridle path or trim his whiskers or fetlocks, I could always do it with scissors. I just wasn't sure that I wanted to put him through the stress that he would obviously experience by working on the problem.

On the other hand, I got to thinking about what might happen if, for some reason, we were forced at some point to use clippers on him. For instance, what would happen if we didn't fix the problem and one day we had to shave him because he needed stitches somewhere? Or what if he was being ridden down the trail or street and he suddenly heard a similar sound? What then? Would he panic and run off or hurt himself or his rider because I hadn't taken the time to work with him?

These were the thoughts going through my mind—the things I considered before making my decision on whether to work with him or not. In the end, as you might have guessed, I came to the conclusion that it's always better to have a horse that's unafraid of something that it might encounter, and so I decided to go ahead and work on the problem.

In the past I had found that, like the mare that was afraid of the spray bottle, one of the best ways to help a horse overcome its fear while causing it the least amount of stress was to work the horse loose in a round pen. Now, the idea behind that is to allow the horse the opportunity to use its flight instinct when things get too scary. With this gelding, if the sound of the clippers frightened him, he could go ahead and run away. Of course, being in the round pen meant that even though he could run, he still couldn't get away from the sound, and that, in itself, was the whole key to the success of this technique. Eventually, if I were quiet and consistent and if I weren't trying to force the noise on him, as would be the case if he were tied, he should be able to get used to the idea of the noise. Hopefully, once he became used to the sound being right there in the round pen with him, he would let me approach him with the clippers and eventually allow me to touch him with them.

However, choosing to carry electric clippers around in a round pen while the horse was running loose was not only not very practical, but also quite dangerous. The chances of either the horse or myself becoming tangled in the electrical cord attached to the clippers were more than just pretty good. In order to use the round pen, I had to find an alternative to using electric clippers. The question then was what I should use.

The answer seemed obvious. All I needed to do was go out and buy some of those newfangled cordless clippers that some veterinarians carry. Surely they would do the job. I soon found that while cordless clippers might have eliminated the problem of becoming tangled in a cord, they posed a couple of other obstacles that rendered them not very practical. First, and most important, was the cost. The cordless clippers that I looked at in the local tack shop were so expensive that I would have had to sell the horse to buy them. The other problem was the fact that they were made so well that they were virtually noiseless. If I had used them, I'm afraid I would have defeated the purpose. After all, before a horse can overcome the fear of a particular noise, it kind of needs to hear the noise it's afraid of.

I began considering other options. I needed to find something that simulated the sound of clippers and at the same time was portable and cordless. After giving the situation a great deal of thought, I finally decided on one tool that had all those qualities. It's seldom, if ever, considered a horse-training device, but it was the one tool that I figured gave me the best chance of getting the job done. The tool was nothing more than a small cordless drill.

My hope that the noise of the drill would be close enough to the sound of the clippers was confirmed a few minutes after I turned the gelding loose in the round pen. He was standing quietly near the gate when I pulled on the trigger that activated the drill motor. He immediately spun and took off running along the rail. As he did, I simply stood in the middle of the pen and held the trigger about halfway down, so that the drill made a constant, high-pitched droning similar to the sound of medium-sized clippers.

I was surprised to see that he only ran for about five minutes before slowing down to a walk and finally coming to a stop. As he did, I let up on the trigger and let him stand without having to listen to the sound of the drill. I went over and petted him for a few seconds before going back to the middle of the pen where, once again, I pulled on the trigger. That time, the gelding only trotted off a few paces before coming to a stop. As he did, I let up on the trigger and walked over to pet him.

He was calming down quite a bit, and this time as I began to back away and pull on the trigger, he barely flinched. Seeing that, I stopped about ten feet from him while I continued to run the drill, and he remained standing in the same spot showing little sign of concern. Once again, I let up on the trigger, walked over to pet him, then backed away and started the drill again. It was apparent that the sound no longer bothered him, at least from a distance, so I saw that as a good opportunity to start moving the sound closer to him. I moved no closer than a foot at a time, alternating running the drill, stopping, and going up to pet him.

Before long, I was standing at his shoulder petting him with one hand and running the drill with the other. As I continued to pet him, I slowly raised the running drill until its side almost touched him. Then I lowered the drill back to my side, let up on the trigger, and backed away for a few seconds. I did this for two reasons. The first was to give him a break from the noise, which after about half an hour can get on your nerves a bit, and the second was to reward him for doing what I was asking—standing still while I ran the thing close to him.

For the next fifteen or twenty minutes, I slowly continued to work the running drill near him until I was finally able to touch him on his shoulder with the side of it. He flinched a little when he felt the vibration of the drill for the first time, but he never tried to run off.

That was the turning point. He was more than willing to pay attention to what I was trying to show him, and the fear he'd shown when we first started had all but disappeared. From that point on, he progressed in leaps and bounds. I was able to slowly work the running drill from his shoulder up to his back, over his sides, and down his legs. I was also, after a time, able to work it up and down the side of his neck, over his cheeks and the bridge of his nose. Finally, after working with him for over an hour, I was even able to reach the area that I'd set out for in the first place—up around his ears and his poll. Our timing was perfect, because I'd just gotten the drill to the area where I'd need to get clippers in order to clip a bridle path when the battery began to lose its charge. As a result, I decided that was as good a time as any to quit for the day.

The next day, having recharged the drill overnight, I took the gelding back to the round pen and started all over. This time, he showed no fear as I pulled on the trigger while I stood in the middle of the pen. Because he was so calm, I was standing at his side within a matter of minutes, running the drill over all the areas that I had when we'd finished the day before, including his face and the area around his ears and poll. Even though he was showing no signs of being troubled by the noise of the drill, I continued to work with him for nearly an hour to make sure that there were no problem areas. It was obvious to me by the end of our session that the noise was no longer a problem for him.

On the third day, I led the gelding out and tied him to the hitch rail just outside the barn door. I brought the drill out and ran it all over him, just as I had in the round pen. He showed no sign of being bothered by the noise, and after a few minutes, I put the drill away and brought out the real clippers. The noise of the clipper motor varied only slightly from sound of the drill motor, and as I approached him with the clippers for the first time, I found that he didn't seem to mind a bit.

Without touching him with the blades, I ran the clippers over all the areas that I'd covered with the drill, only to find that he seemed bored with the whole situation. As a result, after about five minutes I was actually trimming his whiskers, cutting a bridle path, and trimming his fetlocks. The noise of his hair being cut for the first time seemed to bother him some, but not enough to cause him to blow up. After a short time he seemed to take even that noise for granted.

It was a little hard for me to believe how easy it had been to overcome the gelding's fear of clippers. In a relatively short time he'd gone from being completely terrified of the clipper noise to being oblivious to it, even though I hadn't used clippers to help him get over his fear. It was perfect proof of the old man's theory that a horse will learn better by showing him what you want in a way that's easy for him to understand and easy for him to perform. That was certainly the key in this horse's case. By working with him loose in a round pen, I was able to eliminate his fear of the noise by allowing him to take as much time as he needed to get used to it. Once he understood that the noise wasn't going to harm him, he was able to relax and listen to me. On the other hand, had I kept him tied to the hitch rail and tried to force him to accept the noise, he more than likely would have seen my actions as aggression. As a result, he would have fought like crazy either to get away or get me to stop. It would have been much harder for me to gain his trust, if I could have at all. Each time he was approached with clippers after that, he probably would have figured he was going to be in for a fight and responded accordingly.

I guess I was lucky in that I had the opportunity a long time ago to observe and learn about horses from a man who gave more thought to them than he did to himself. He showed me how to avoid fighting with them by putting myself in the horse's place and then working from that point of view.

It seems to me that the whole idea behind working with horses should come down to a few simple things. As horse people we should try to take our horse's perspective into consideration each and every time we work with him. We should try to work through problems *with* the horse and in ways that cause the least amount of trauma to all parties involved. And, when it's all said and done, both horse and rider should have no hard feelings toward one another. Only then will we have been able to master the true tricks of the trade.

PART FOUR

The Gift

10

The Gift

It was two days after my graduation from high school, and I was standing in the fading sun of early evening watching a filling station attendant grudgingly put three dollars' worth of ethyl gas into the tank of my father's light-brown Olds. I'd borrowed the car so I could take my girlfriend out to a movie and humbly apologize to her for the argument we'd gotten into on graduation night about which parties to attend that evening. On the front seat of the Olds sat two flowers that had cost me nearly seventy-five cents apiece and whose name I couldn't pronounce. They were wrapped up in thin white paper and were intended as a peace offering, which would hopefully help to get the evening off on the right foot.

I was admiring the large, Nevada-shaped grease stain on the back of the attendant's shirt and, at the same time, trying desperately to think of a witty opening line for my girlfriend, when I heard something that completely broke my concentration. It was a sound I hadn't heard in over a year and a half but which was so familiar to me that I knew right away what it was.

"That'll be three bucks," the young fellow's voice squeaked, as he finished putting the gas in my tank and returned the hose to its position on the pump.

I dug three one-dollar bills from inside my new wallet (a graduation present) and placed them in the palm of his outstretched hand. As I looked up, I could see the source of the familiar sound slowly coming into view. It was still a quarter-mile away, but its shape was unmistakable. It was the shape of a well-worn 1949 Ford pickup truck.

The clanging and banging noise it made as it rolled laboriously down the road told me that it belonged to none other than the old man.

Shortly before I entered the eighth grade five years earlier, our family had moved from the house where I'd lived since I was born to a neighboring town nearly fifteen miles from the old man's horse operation. Because of that, my visits to his place and my time spent working with him and his horses had become sporadic at best. In fact, it had been nearly a year and a half since I'd worked my last horse for him, and sadly, I hadn't seen him since. As I stood watching his beat up old truck bounce haplessly down the road, I found myself hoping he'd pull into the filling station. I was hoping he'd stop for the simple reason that I wanted to say hello to him and ask how things had been going.

I stood by the open door of my dad's Olds and watched as the old truck rolled closer. Then, without even slowing down, it rolled past.

Well, I thought to myself, maybe next time. With that, I climbed in the car, started it up, and pulled away from the pump. I hadn't even gotten to the station's entrance, however, when through my open window I found I could hear the sound of the old truck heading back in my direction. I quickly pulled my car off to the side just in time to see the old truck veer into the filling station and slide toward the side of the station where an air hose lay half-coiled on the ground. The old truck squeaked to a reluctant stop beside the hose, then wheezed and coughed as the old man shut off the motor and climbed out of the cab.

I quickly got out of the car and made my way over to the side of the truck where the old man was crouched down, filling the front tire with air. It was only as I approached and was getting ready to say hello that it suddenly dawned on me that in all the time I'd known him, I'd never called him by name. I never called him mister this or sir that, and I certainly never referred to him as the "old man." Looking back, I couldn't recall him ever addressing me either. I suppose the reason was that most of the time we worked together it was just him and me. Very seldom was anyone else around, so I knew that when he was talking, he was probably talking to me. If I was talking, I was probably talking to him. There'd never been any reason for us to refer to each other by name, and as I approached, I simply couldn't bring myself to do it.

"Maybe it's time for a new truck," I quipped, as if the last time I'd seen him was just yesterday. "I hear they make some new ones every year."

"Naw," he slowly shook his head without even looking up. "It'll be another three years before this one is broke in good. I'd hate to quit on her before I got my money's worth."

"I suppose that's true," I nodded. "How have you been?"

"About as good as I get," he said, putting his left hand on the fender of the truck and pushing himself to a standing position. It was only then that I got a good look at him and what I saw disturbed me. He had lost a tremendous amount of weight and his face was pale and thin. He had large, dark circles under his eyes and about a week's worth of growth on his beard. It appeared as though he was having a hard time breathing and standing up straight, and as he started to make his way around the front of the truck, he burst into an uncontrollable, terrible-sounding cough. The cough lasted for several minutes, causing him to double over, and was punctuated by him spitting into the nearby grass.

"Are you okay?" I asked, following him around the front of the truck.

"Yeah," he grunted, crouching down to fill the other front tire with air. "I've got this damn cold I can't seem to get rid of. What about you?" He glanced up in my direction. "Don't they have any barbers up there where you live?"

He was referring to the fact that my hair had gotten considerably longer since the last time he'd seen me.

"There are," I smiled. "I guess I just haven't been to one in a while."

"I guess," he grunted. "You're starting to look like one of them hippies that I seen on TV. The next thing I know, you'll be wearing sandals on your feet and beads around your neck."

"I don't think so," I told him with a smile.

"I hope not," he burst into another coughing episode that lasted about as long as the first one. "You been working any horses?" he asked, as soon as he was able to catch his breath.

"Not really," I said, apologetically. "I've kind of been busy playing music lately. I'm playing drums in a band."

"A band," he said, with a bit of surprise in his voice. "It ain't one of them rock-and-roll outfits, is it?"

"Well, kind of," I replied.

"Lord help us," he shook his head.

For the next half-hour or so, we visited about various things, most of which had to do with horses, and during our conversation he told me that he no longer owned his little place. He said that there had been an awful lot of development going on in that area over the past few years, and as a result, the taxes on his place had skyrocketed. They had gotten so high, in fact, that he hadn't been able to pay them for a couple of years. The place had been foreclosed on by the county a couple of months earlier and sold at auction. He told me that all he had left from the place was his saddle, a few other little pieces of tack, and his chair—the one he kept in the tack room. Everything else was gone.

"It doesn't really matter though," he said, trying to force a smile. "It was getting to be too much work for me anyhow."

He suddenly switched gears, as if trying to get off the subject, and began to ask about what I'd been up to lately. I happily told him about the band I was playing in and how I had graduated from high school a couple of days before. I also told him about the girl I'd been going out with and the argument we'd had on graduation night.

"I'm taking her to a movie tonight," I told him, as we leaned against the fender of his old truck. "I got her some flowers, too. Hopefully that'll help make up for the fight we had the other night."

"Well," he said, looking out across a nearby hay field, "giving her flowers sure couldn't hurt. It's been my experience that just about everyone likes getting a gift every now and again." He pushed himself away from the truck and slowly made his way over to the driver's-side door.

"I remember the best gift I ever got," he said, as he jerked on the door handle, opening the door. "I got it when I was just a kid and I kept it for years and years."

"Really?" I questioned, surprised that the old man could actually be sentimental enough to hold on to anything for an extended period of time.

"I finally decided to give it away though," he said, as he climbed behind the wheel and slammed the door behind him. "It had gotten to where I couldn't really use it much anymore, and I didn't want it to go to waste. I gave it to a fellow who I thought might get some use out of it."

"No kidding," I said, as he reached down and made his first attempt to start the old Ford. "What was . . ."

"You should probably get going," he interrupted, pumping the gas pedal several times then making a second attempt at getting the truck to start. "You don't want to be late for your movie."

The old truck suddenly wheezed and coughed to life, shaking and rattling as it did. The old man sat quietly with both hands on the wheel for several seconds before slowly turning toward me and sticking his right hand out the window. It was the only time that I could recall in all the years I'd known him that he ever offered to shake my hand.

"I'm heading up to Montana," he said, as I took hold of his hand and shook it. "I'm gonna look up some old friends, if they're still alive, and maybe do a little fishing." He paused, returning his right hand to its position on the steering wheel and once again looking out across the nearby hay field.

"You know something," he said, after several seconds had passed, "if playing that rock-and-roll music ever loses its shine for you, you might want to try your hand at horses again." He ground the transmission into reverse. "You always seemed to have the heart for it."

He looked over at me as the old pickup slowly backed away. "I'll see ya," he said, half-shouting over the noise of the engine.

"See ya," I responded.

About six months later I was once again sitting at a filling station putting gas in my father's car. The sun hadn't been out since early that afternoon and it had been replaced by heavy clouds carrying the season's first snow. In fact, I had just pulled into the filling station when the first few flakes began falling. I paid for my gas and was opening the car door when from down the road the familiar sound of the old man's truck came rumbling in my direction. I stood by the open car door as the old truck slowly came into view, veered into the station's lot, and squeaked to a stop beside one of the gas pumps. I immediately began to make my way over to the truck, but stopped short as the driver's-side door swung open.

Much to my surprise, from out of the truck crawled a very large man with a heavy beard and long, greasy hair, dressed in dirty jeans and a black leather vest with the logo of the local motorcycle club sewn on the back. It was only then that I noticed the Harley-Davidson motorcycle decal in the truck's back window. It was obvious that the truck no longer belonged to the old man, but as I stood looking at it and the fellow who appeared to be its owner, I couldn't help but wonder why the old man had sold it in the first place. After all, I didn't think he'd ever get rid of it. Finally, my curiosity got the better of me and I made my way over to the fellow.

"You don't see many like this anymore," I said, referring to the pickup as I approached. "Have you had it long?"

"About two months," he replied.

"Do you mind me asking where you got it?" I questioned.

"An estate sale," he said bluntly. "Some old guy died and they sold his stuff so's they could pay to plant him."

"An estate sale," I said, taken aback.

"Yeah," he grunted, "there wasn't much there though. This old Ford was the only thing worth buying. The rest of the stuff was mostly junk."

As I turned to walk back to my car, I could feel my heart sink. I couldn't believe it. The old man was gone.

I would love to be able to say that the old man's passing had such a profound effect on me that I abandoned my attempt to become a professional musician and threw all my energies back into working with horses. Unfortunately, that wasn't the case. In fact, as time went on, just the opposite was true. I found that even though my love for animals was just as strong as it ever was, my desire to work with them was almost completely gone. It was almost as though the old man had somehow taken that along with him when he went.

For example, the girl I was going out with at the time owned a horse of her own. She not only worked with the mare nearly every day, but she also spent a lot of time trail riding and going to local horse shows. As for me, I seldom, if ever, offered to help her with the horse and, in fact, often went out of my way to avoid even the slightest contact with the mare.

As time went on and my girlfriend and I eventually went our separate ways, my connection with horses slipped further and further away. I was devoting much of my time to playing music in various bands, often spending days or even weeks on the road, and in my down time I worked for the local Firestone tire store. My primary job with Firestone was traveling to outlying farms and ranches to do on-site tractor tire repair and replacement. Oddly enough, it was this job that provided the catalyst for my return to horses.

I was just finishing up a tire repair at a small farm when I happened to notice a middle-aged woman trying to catch a horse in a nearby corral. The corral was about forty feet in diameter, and the woman was having no luck whatsoever getting close to the gelding. While I finished my repairs, the woman apparently tried everything she could think of to get the horse caught, including hiding the halter behind her back, trying to pin him in a corner, and coaxing and bribing him with grain and other treats. She even attempted to herd him into a box stall in the barn attached to the corral. Nothing worked. By the time I'd finished and put all my tools away, over an hour had passed without her getting within so much as six feet of the horse.

Frankly, I don't know what got into me, but I soon found myself standing next to the corral and asking the woman if she minded if I went in and tried to catch the horse.

"Be my guest," she said, obviously discouraged with the horse's behavior. "I'm sure not having much luck with him."

"I don't know if I will either," I said, as I slid between the rails of the fence and took the halter and lead rope that she held in her outstretched hand. "It's been a while since I worked any horses."

With that, I slowly began to make my way toward the horse, only to receive the same response that the woman had. The horse simply turned his butt to me and began to trot off. Seeing that and remembering something the old man had shown me years ago about working with a hard-to-catch horse, I began to twirl the lead rope at my side. The reason for doing this, as the old man had explained, was to put pressure on the horse as he moved away, thereby making it harder for him to go away from me than it was to stand still. The horse responded by taking off at a dead run around the inside of the corral. He made several very fast laps before stopping in a corner with his head over the fence. As soon as he stopped, I quit twirling the rope, releasing the pressure, and stood as quietly as I could.

After giving him a little time to rest and think about the situation, I began to approach him. He looked as if he was getting ready to run off, but instead he turned and threw a worried glance in my direction. As soon as he glanced at me, I stopped my approach and took a step or two backwards to reward him for a proper response—standing still and looking in my direction instead of running away. I gave him a couple more minutes to think about it before once again making my way toward him. I had only taken two or three very slow steps in his direction when he suddenly turned and faced me. A bit surprised at this reaction from him, I stopped dead in my tracks for a second or two, then stepped backwards, again rewarding him for a proper response. As I stepped backwards, he stepped toward me, matching me step for step.

This went on for about five minutes—me stepping toward him, him stepping toward me, and me backing away. Before I knew it, he was standing with his nose almost touching my chest. At that point, I slowly raised my hand and petted him on his forehead and neck while I eased my way around to his left side. Once there, I continued to pet him with one hand while showing him the halter with the other. He appeared oblivious to the halter, which prompted me to slip it over his nose and slowly buckle it in place. Once the halter was on him, I gave him a few more pats on the neck before leading him over to the woman, who by now had made her way back inside the corral.

"I've never seen anything like that before," she said, as I handed her the lead rope. "It almost looked like he was trying to catch you. How did you do that?"

"Well, actually it's something that was shown to me a long time ago," I replied, trying to hold back an exuberant smile. "I'm glad I remembered how to do it. I wasn't sure if I would or not."

"Well, I'll certainly say this," she said, quietly stroking the horse's forehead. "For not having caught a horse in a while, you sure made it look easy. You must just have a gift when it comes to things like that."

"I don't know about that," I said, making my way out of the corral. "I think it was mostly just luck."

With that, I made my way over to my truck and was soon heading back to the shop. It was strange, but as I drove I had this overwhelming urge to swing down the road where the old man's little horse ranch used to be. It had been years since I'd been out that way, and because I'd finished all my service calls and was an hour ahead of schedule, I figured it'd be okay to take the five-mile detour that would put me in that vicinity.

It wasn't long before I found myself turning down the old familiar road that eventually took me to the entrance to his place. As I drove, I couldn't help but notice all the changes in the area. I could recall when the road was little more than one lane of dirt and gravel, skirted by hay fields and ditches full of willow bushes. That was no longer the case. It was now a paved two-lane street with yellow stripes down the middle. The willows and the hay fields were gone and in their place were rows of condominiums and houses, complete with children's swing sets, patios, barbecues, and garages.

I slowed the truck as I approached the spot where the gate to the old man's place used to be, and much to my surprise, I found it still intact and standing right where it had always been. I turned the truck into the driveway, stopping just short of the old wooden gate, which now sported a large red-and-white "No Trespassing" sign, and shut off the motor. I sat for a few minutes, assessing the damage to the area from all the development, and came to the conclusion that the old man's place had fared pretty well. The front and south pastures were still intact and even had some of the fences (most of which I'd helped to put up nearly eleven years earlier) still standing. There also appeared to be a small portion of the old riding arena fence still standing.

Unfortunately, I was able to see the arena fence because the main barn, which the arena had been behind, had been torn down. In fact, as I looked up the quarter-mile-long driveway, now overgrown with weeds, it was difficult to tell where any of the buildings once stood. The old barn with the leaky roof, the seemingly massive hay barn, the chicken coop that once doubled as a bunkhouse, and even

the wooden round pen where I spent countless hours watching the old man work his magic on horse after horse, were all gone. Gone without a trace.

I sat for just a little while longer, looking back on the time I had spent with the old man, when something dawned on me. I vaguely remembered the last time I saw him, when he mentioned to me almost in passing a gift that he had received as a child. He never actually told me what that gift was, but he did tell me that he had kept it for many years, and when he could no longer use it, he gave it to someone else so that it wouldn't go to waste. Ironically, only an hour before, a woman had suggested that perhaps I had a "gift" because of the way I was able to catch a horse that didn't want to be caught. I suddenly found it very interesting that she had used that particular term to describe what had happened between me and that horse, and it was something that got me to thinking.

It got me thinking about all the things I'd seen the old man do with horses all those years ago. Things like catching the uncatchable, loading the unloadable, and training the untrainable. Although his methods may have varied somewhat in each case, his attitude never did. He always took into consideration how the horse perceived the situation, then tried to work from that perspective. He always worked with quiet persistence and patience and never bullied or forced an animal into submission, no matter what the circumstance. He seemed to be a master at knowing how to work at the horse's own speed. He taught as fast or as slow as the horse could learn and got as much out of each session as he possibly could without stressing the horse or losing the horse's attention.

While I was thinking about these things and all of the horses I'd watched the old man work, something else came back to me. I recalled one horse that the old man had been working with for quite some time. The horse was a paint gelding that had been terribly abused by its previous owner and didn't appear to be responding to any of the handling or techniques that the old man tried. Several months had passed and the gelding didn't appear to be making any progress. One day I mentioned to the old man that the gelding appeared to be a lost cause, and his response to my statement took me by surprise.

"There are times," I remember him saying, "when you've been in the desert so long, you don't know when you've stumbled into an oasis, even when you're knee deep in water. The longer you stay there, though, the more likely you are to take a drink." He smiled ever so slightly. "That little fellow just doesn't realize he's in an oasis . . . yet."

After I remembered that, it finally dawned on me what the old man had been doing all those years. He had been providing an oasis for those horses that needed one. He'd found a way to help the horses he came in contact with by opening the lines of communication between him and them. He'd been able to prove, time and time again, that you didn't have to beat a horse to get it to work for you. And even more importantly, he had proved, at least to me, that a good horse is always a good horse, no matter what color, size, or sex it happens to be, or what background it happens to come from.

I came to understand that the gift the old man had talked about the last time I'd seen him wasn't something that you could physically touch or hold or see. It was more than that. It was something that he carried inside. The gift that he had possessed since he was a child and that he wanted to pass along was simply his love and understanding for the animals he had spent his entire life working with and helping.

The old man told me, the last time I spoke with him, that he had passed the gift along to a fellow that he thought might be able to get some use out of it. I happen to know for a fact that not only did that fellow, indeed, get some use out of it, but now, perhaps, so can you.

Index